TRADING
MADE EASY

The definitive beginners' guide to profiting
in all market conditions

Todd M. Mitchell

Printed in the United States of America

First Printing, 2016

ISBN: 978-0692788721

30100 Telegraph Rd, Bingham Farms, MI 48025

www.tradingconceptsinc.com

Welcome to Your Future

If you're reading this book you've already made a great decision: to learn more about an opportunity. That opportunity is trading the markets and with that comes exciting possibilities, the best of which is to increase your earning potential. With this book, the basic ingredients for successful and profitable trading are now at your fingertips.

What to Expect

In this book you will become familiar with how trading the markets works, from basic terminology to charting market trends. I want you to finish this book with a vision of the enormous potential in trading the markets and the confidence to dig deeper into the world of trading. Whether you want to increase your income, grow your savings or change your lifestyle, this book is just the beginning. The information that follows can change your life, as it has for me and many of my students.

What Is Trading the Markets?

In the jargon of the financial world, to trade the markets simply means to voluntarily exchange (buy and sell) financial instruments with other traders. Most traders participate in the markets to profit from short- or medium-term fluctuations in the market value (price) of a financial instrument.

As with any profession or hobby, trading has its own lingo—and the more you understand it, the better you'll understand the concepts and strategies shared in this book. At the end of this book you'll find a glossary of terms. You can flip to the glossary as you read in order to gain a better understanding of the content within. You can also read through it first to familiarize yourself with trading lingo. As you read through this book, remember: if you come across an unfamiliar word or phrase, refer to the glossary for clarification.

Why Trading Is the BEST Job in the World

There is no other career more lucrative than trading; in fact, traders can make more than movie stars! It doesn't happen overnight, but remember, many movie stars started out waiting tables. Regardless of what your current job is, where you come from, where you live or what kind of car you drive, you have the opportunity to learn to trade the markets profitably. With patience, diligence and the right coaching, you can make it happen. You can reach your goals and turn your dreams into reality—just like I've been able to do!

More Good News

You don't need to have an "in" or a middleman in order to trade (or to trade profitably for that matter), and you certainly don't have to be an expert economist or a financial wizard to trade the markets. With the right knowledge and practice, you can trade just like the folks on Wall Street (maybe not at their price range right away, but that's okay).

There are many advantages to trading:

- You can work from home.
- You are your own boss.
- You get to choose your trading hours, from the time of day you work to the duration of your workday.
- Low start-up cost
- No permits or licenses required
- No inventory
- No overhead
- No employees

To be a profitable trader, all you need is a computer with an internet connection, a desire to learn and a mentor—yes, that's right, a mentor. Someone to teach you the ropes, keep you from developing bad habits, and guide you through this exciting journey. This is what I'm here for. Are you ready? Let's get started!

TODD MITCHELL

Table of Contents

Welcome to Your Future 5
    What to Expect...5
    What Is Trading the Markets? 5
    Why Trading Is the BEST Job in the World..............6

A Note From the Author 13

Chapter 1: Market Basics...17
    Who Can Trade the Markets? 18
    What Exactly Do People Trade?.............................18
    Where Is Trading Done?.......................................18
    U.S. Stock Exchanges..19
    What's a Bull and Bear Market? 23
        Bull Market...24
        Bear Market 24

Chapter 2: Getting Started..25
    Minimum Investing Amounts 26
    Getting Personal...26
        Personal Traits for Trading Successfully..................27
    The Psychology of Trading 28
    The Danger of Emotions 30
    Work Toward Continuous Self-Improvement..........31
    Getting Physical...31
    Determining Your Goals......................................31
    Tips for Setting Goals 32
        Tips for Achieving Your Personal Goals 33
        Tips for Achieving Your Trading Goals..................33

Chapter 3: Trading Basics..35

The Four Most Common Types of Traders 35
    Scalpers 35
    Day Traders 35
    Swing Traders 36
    Position Traders 36
Trading Styles & Market Time Frames 37
Time Frames Used for Trading 38
Fundamental Versus Technical Analysis 39
    Fundamental Analysis—Economics and News 39
    Technical Analysis—Chart Reading 39

Chapter 4: Going Deeper Into the World of Trading 41
Selling Short 41
Getting Technical 44
Charts: I Have Some Explaining to Do 44
    Bar Charts 44
    Candlestick Charts 46
Up and Down, Bull or Bear? 49
    Trend Lingo 49
Charts and Trading Trends Go Hand in Hand 50
What's Up With Charts? 50
    Uptrends 51
    Downtrend 51
    Sideways 52
Support and Resistance 52
Resistance Becoming Support 54
Support Becoming Resistance 54
Sideways Market or Trading Range 55
What Is Price Action? 56
Moving Averages and Indicators 58
    Simple Moving Average 58

Exponential Moving Average 58
Key Moving Average Concepts to Understand...........59
What Is a Technical Indicator? 61
Moving Average Convergence-Divergence 63
Relative Strength Index 64
Stochastics 65
What Is Volatility? 66

Chapter 5: Creating Yourself as a Trader......................68
Common Trading Styles 69
Breakout Trading 69
Retracement and/or Pullback Trading......................70
Trend Trading 71
Countertrend Trading..72
Trend Trading vs. Countertrend Trading 72
Managing Your Money...73
The True Essence of Money Management Is Managing
Risk...74
Managing Risk with Stop Losses 75

Chapter 6: Becoming the Trader You Want to Be 77
Twenty Rules for Trading Success 77
Twenty Truisms Applicable to Trading 81
Final Review 83
What Type of Trader Will You Be? 86
The YOU Assessment: Questions for Maximizing
Your Trading Potential.......................................86
Section 1: Questions About Your Personality 90
Section 2: Questions About Your Comfort Level.....91
Section 3: Questions About Your Time Commitment
....93

Section 4: Questions About Your Energy Level.......93
Section 5: Questions About Your Capital
Commitment 94
Section 6: Questions About Your Wants, Needs and
Desires 95

A Final Note from Todd 99

About Trading Concepts 101

Testimonials.. 103

Glossary of Terms... 109

A Note From the Author

First off, I want to applaud you again for taking the time to not only get this book, but to read what I'm going to teach you. I truly believe that this book will help change you and your family's financial future for the better. At the very least it will show you what your potential is, if you have the desire to follow through with the lessons inside.

Before we get started on your journey, however, I want to tell you a little bit about my journey and help you understand the reasons I became a mentor to traders and would-be traders just like you.

My interest in the futures and stock market, which quickly grew to fascination, began when I manually updated my father's charts on a daily basis in the 1980s. Eventually, I began reading about, studying and researching the markets more seriously, back in 1987 while I was still in college. One year later I started to actively trade with real money. After graduating from college with a business finance degree in 1990, I decided to trade full-time since I had already seen firsthand how much money could be made. During this time, I also met with a few would-be mentors to hone my skills. Sadly, one of these mentors wasn't the trader he presented himself to be and while I knew better than to follow his advice, I saw many others who didn't know better and that made a huge impression on me.

After I had a few successful trading years under my belt and I'd tweaked my strategies with all that I'd learned, I decided to use my extensive knowledge and experience to launch Trading Concepts to help other traders.

I was fortunate that after forming Trading Concepts in 1994, we quickly established a reputation as one of the industry's finest educational companies due to the powerful trading strategies that I had developed and the positive results my students were experiencing. By combining powerful stock, options, futures and forex trading strategies with sound trade and money management techniques, I was able to help individual traders gain the power and knowledge base that before had only been available to professional traders.

Now, I teach people all over the world, including new traders, experienced traders and everyone in between, how to succeed in today's markets. I demonstrate step-by-step trading strategies in clear, concise terms, using effective analogies and examples through all of my educational trading programs. My goal is to teach all of my students the correct mindset and money management techniques for trading, whether you're a beginner, intermediate or more experienced trader. Through helping students, I show the gratitude I have for my dad who introduced me to the markets and taught me many valuable trading lessons that I still use today.

You should also understand that I literally (yes, *literally*) breathe, eat, drink and sleep the markets. Trading is and has always been the only job for me. I have yet to hear about another profession more intriguing, exciting or potentially profitable than being a successful trader! While reading this book you'll see that I truly have a love for the markets and teaching that echoes throughout all of my work.

The bottom line is this: you do not have to be a rocket scientist to be a good trader. With the proper discipline, patience, a strong desire to succeed and a sound trading methodology, you _can_ be successful in this business. If I can do it successfully, YOU can certainly do it too!

Yours in trading success,

Todd Mitchell

Todd Mitchell

CEO and Founder of Trading Concepts

Chapter 1: Market Basics

Many people think the terms *trading* and *investing* mean the same thing. Yes, both can have something to do with the stock market—but that's where the similarity ends.

Investing is essentially about putting your money in the trust of someone else and hoping they'll grow it to a larger amount in the future, as in months or years or decades from now. An investment can be made in a bank account, a stock, bonds, CDs, mutual funds or similar instruments. For most people, investing is a passive activity. You allocate the money once and then cross your fingers.

Trading, on the other hand, is an active process. When you learn a set of trading rules and strategies, you can monitor the markets in just a few minutes (depending on what type of trading you decide to do) to make new decisions on whether to buy or sell. When you *trade*, you can literally create wealth and income now—*today*—not in the distant future.

The reason this distinction matters so much is that investors don't need to understand the markets the same way traders do. Traders are going to be profiting off every turn the markets take—and they will do so in several markets. This means they need to understand the ins and outs of the markets—at least, they do if they want to be profitable.

Who Can Trade the Markets?

Anyone with some money to invest can trade the markets. Whether you want to trade the markets a couple hours a day, half a day or all day is up to you. This can be a part-time endeavor or your own full-time business. The opportunities are endless. However, I do NOT recommend that you start trading unless you have the proper foundation of knowledge and a mentor. In Chapter 2, I'll talk about how much money you should start with but that too is flexible.

What Exactly Do People Trade?

In today's world you can trade just about anything. Anything that is traded in the financial markets is called a security (financial instrument). Most securities can also be traded as derivatives. A *derivative* is a financial contract that *derives* its value from the performance of another entity such as an asset, index or interest rate, called the "underlying" factors. Futures and options are both derivatives.

Where Is Trading Done?

Trading can be done anywhere in the world with a computer, tablet or phone and an internet connection. The exchanges are the institutions that electronically record all the shares of stocks, options contracts, bonds, forex, commodities, ETFs, etc., that are bought and sold. The exchanges are where buyers connect with sellers. You can buy and sell on these exchanges through an online broker (I will direct you to those in Chapter 2). There are more than 100 exchanges around the world.

U.S. Stock Exchanges

- Boston Options Exchange (BOX)
- Chicago Board Options Exchange (CBOE)
- Chicago Climate Exchange (CCX; parent company of the Chicago Climate Futures Exchange, European Climate Exchange and Insurance Futures Exchange)
- Chicago Mercantile Exchange (CME)
- Chicago Stock Exchange (CHX)
- Currenex (currency exchange)
- ICE (Intercontinental Exchange)
- International Securities Exchange
- Iowa Electronic Markets
- Minneapolis Grain Exchange (MGEX)
- NASDAQ OMX
- NASDAQ Stock Market
- National Stock Exchange (NSX; formerly Cincinnati Stock Exchange)
- New York Stock Exchange (NYSE; merged with Euronext)
- OneChicago (OCX; joint venture of CME, CBOT and CBOE)
- OTC Bulletin Board
- Philadelphia Stock Exchange (PHLX)
- Pink Sheets (formerly the National Quotation Bureau)

- San Diego Stock Exchange

The two most well-known stock exchanges in the United States are:

- New York Stock Exchange (NYSE), founded in 1792

- Nasdaq, founded in 1971

Today, most trades are executed electronically and even stocks themselves are almost always held in electronic form, not as physical certificates.

But trading is not just about stocks. There are multiple markets or "trading vehicles" from which to choose. These may also be referred to as *financial instruments*. All are easily accessible from home to anyone with a computer and an internet connection. All things traded on these markets are referred to as securities.

What Markets Can Be Traded?

Here is a list of the main markets from which we can all profit:

- Stocks
- ETFs
- Options
- Stock index futures (E-Minis)
- Bonds
- Commodities
- Forex currency pairs

20

Stock Market: The stock market is where shares of publicly held companies are bought and sold. It's also known as the equity market. Stocks are traded through exchanges, such as the New York Stock Exchange (NYSE) and the Nasdaq (NASDAQ). If you want to know how the stock market is performing, you can consult an index of stocks for the whole market or for a segment of the market. Examples include the Dow Jones Industrial Average (DJIA), Nasdaq index, Russell 2000, Standard and Poor's 500 and Morgan Stanley Europe, Australasia and Far East index.

ETF Market: ETFs are securities that closely resemble index funds but can be bought and sold just like stocks. They represent a basket of securities that you can buy and sell whenever the stock exchanges are open. ETFs allow traders and investors a convenient way to purchase a broad assortment of securities in a single transaction. Essentially, ETFs offer the convenience of a stock along with the diversification of a mutual fund.

Options Market: Options are financial derivatives that represent a contract sold by one party (option writer) to another party (option holder). The contract offers the buyer the right, but not the obligation, to buy (call) or sell (put) a security or other financial asset at an agreed-upon price (the strike price) during a certain period of time or on a specific date (exercise date).

Call options give the option to buy at a certain price, so the buyer would want the stock to go up. Put options give the option to sell at a certain price, so the buyer would want the stock to go down.

Futures Market: A marketplace where buyers and sellers come together to trade futures and options contracts on derivatives including interest rates, equity indexes (e-mini futures), foreign exchanges, energy, agricultural commodities and metals. E-mini futures are contracts to buy or sell the value of a specific stock index at a specific price on a specific date in the future. Traders trade e-mini futures primarily to try to profit from speculating on the price fluctuations of the stock market or protect themselves from changes in the price of the underlying indexes. Pension and mutual fund managers typically use e-mini futures for managing risk and hedging portfolios. E-mini futures are one-fifth the size and closely follow the price movement of their respective indexes. E-mini futures contracts are traded completely electronically.

Bond Market: Bonds are debt investments in which an investor loans money to an entity (corporate or government) that borrows the funds for a defined period of time at a fixed interest rate. To finance a variety of projects and activities companies, municipalities, states and governments use bonds. Bonds are commonly referred to as fixed-income securities and are one of the three main asset classes, along with stocks and cash equivalents.

The main categories of bonds are corporate bonds, municipal bonds and U.S. treasury bonds, notes and bills, which are collectively referred to as simply *treasuries*.

Commodities Market: Commodities are raw material or primary agricultural products that are bought and sold on an exchange (i.e., the Chicago Mercantile Exchange (CME) and/or the Intercontinental Exchange (ICE)). Examples of commodities include grains, gold, beef, oil and natural gas. Commodities are traded in the pits at the exchanges and/or may be traded electronically through a broker.

Forex Market: The forex market facilitates the exchange of one currency for another. Forex traders attempt to take advantage of the fluctuations in exchange rates by buying or selling individual currencies to speculate on the future value of one currency relative to another. The forex market is the largest and most traded financial market in the world. There is no central marketplace. Transactions are conducted through dealers over-the-counter, for the most part, electronically, within a network of banks.

Currencies are always traded in pairs, with many potential combinations available, only some of which are very liquid.

What's a Bull and Bear Market?

These two terms are probably the most common in trading the markets. Hearing them gives you an automatic understanding of the strategies you'll likely use from one trading day to the next.

Bull Market

A bull market is a market in which prices are rising, encouraging buying. This term is most often used to refer to the stock market, but can be applied to anything that is traded, such as bonds, currencies and commodities.

Bear Market

A bear market is a market in which prices are falling, encouraging selling. A bear market can also be described as a general decline in the stock market over a period of time.

The use of *bull* and *bear* to describe markets comes from the way the animals attack their opponents. A bull thrusts its horns up into the air while a bear swipes its paws down. These actions are metaphors for the movement of a market. If the trend is up, it's a bull market. If the trend is down, it's a bear market. Either way, you need to have the right strategies in place to avoid getting gouged.

Chapter 2: Getting Started

Many new traders, when cracking open a trading book for the first time, want to immediately start with the strategies. After all, that's the fun part, right? The part that's going to make you rich? Well, not exactly.

You have to build the proper foundation before you can find and tweak a strategy that suits you. If you skip ahead, you're building your trading future on a foundation of ever-shifting sand, and that's not going to get you very far.

Earlier in the book, I mentioned that you would need a computer with an internet connection, some money to invest and an online broker in order to get started. Those are only the minimum requirements for anyone. To be a successful trader, you also need training, time, patience, discipline, a positive mental attitude and a strong desire to succeed.

Once the market trading process and concepts are familiar to you, I recommend that you spend time educating yourself further. Think of trading like you would any professional career change. You wouldn't decide to go from being a lawyer to a doctor without the right training, practice and experience behind you. At least, I *hope* you wouldn't. And if you tried—you'd likely end up in jail.

So I'll say it again: I recommend that you **do not begin trading unless you have had some training and practice.**

Wait to begin trading until you've reached a place where you have learned enough to feel comfortable placing trades, managing your risk and recognizing real opportunities. You can then apply your knowledge by paper trading. Paper trading, also known as simulated trading, is a method of practicing or rehearsing your trading skills before using real funds to invest/trade.

Minimum Investing Amounts

Traders are always asking me how much money they need to get started. The minimum amount can range from $500 to $5,000. How much exactly will depend on what market you are looking to trade and your broker's minimum requirements. Please remember, you should not trade with money that is needed to maintain your daily living. It's best to set aside extra money just for trading.

Here are some online brokers I recommend:

- **TradeStation**: www.tradestation.com
- **Interactive Brokers**: www.interactivebrokers.com
- **Thinkorswim/TD Ameritrade**: www.thinkorswim.com
- **Scottrade**: www.scottrade.com

Getting Personal

Before any trading begins, it will serve you well to understand what personal traits are good for traders to have, the psychology of trading and why goal setting is important.

Personal Traits for Trading Successfully

The following traits are very important for you to understand and, if you don't already have them, to develop. I suggest you try to adhere to them to become a truly successful trader. These traits, partnered with the proper psychology and realistic goals, can make a difference in your overall trading/investing performance.

- The ability to act on your decisions
- The ability to accept responsibility for your actions
- Patience
- Emotional detachment from the markets
- The ability to accept risk and take losses (you'll never be right 100 percent of the time)
- Concentration
- Independent and creative thinking
- The ability to develop insight and proper course of action in various market situations
- Self-control
- The ability to adapt quickly to changing market conditions (i.e., being flexible)
- Knowledge
- Acceptance of your inability to control the market's movements (the market is always right)
- Persistence
- The ability to function in both structured and unstructured environments (up, down and sideways markets)

- A commitment and ability to focus on the task at hand
- The ability to manage your stress effectively. Without this power, you cannot strive and survive in this business.
- Self-discipline
- Decisiveness
- Maintaining a positive mental attitude
- Consistency in applying your trading rules

We could all stand to improve on at least one of the traits above. If you read any of those traits and realized that there are some specific areas you need to work on, I encourage you to do so. There are books on just about every topic these days. Or you could do an internet search for articles written by qualified professionals.

The Psychology of Trading

Thoughts are very powerful things. The thoughts we allow to occupy our minds will determine our mindset. A trader's mindset can be their most important edge or their largest liability.

> *"If you think you can, or if you think you can't, you are right."*
> --Henry Ford

Within you lies the power to determine what your mindset will be. Thoughts affect feelings and actions, which is why you must manage them carefully in the world of trading.

What I'm talking about here is our psychological makeup. You must overcome any and all psychological pitfalls if you want to achieve profits and attain longevity in the markets.

Think about it this way: it's the psychology of traders that moves the markets to begin with, and that's why your thoughts and feelings are important. Whether you're a day trader or a long-term trader, your thinking and emotions will affect your trading.

Your thoughts control how you feel; thus thinking positively leads to feeling **POSITIVE,** which gives you a greater chance in being successful in the markets.

Here's a quote that conveys how your feelings can affect your decision-making process:

You are totally responsible for your actions 100 percent of the time. Being accountable for your actions will allow you to review your shortcomings and improve. This is a very important trait for long-term trading success. Never blame anybody else.

> *"When you are feeling gloomy, everything seems to go wrong;*
> *When you're feeling cheerful, everything seems right.*
> *However,*
> *If you don't like the way you are feeling,*
> *You can change the way you are thinking."*
> **--Unknown**

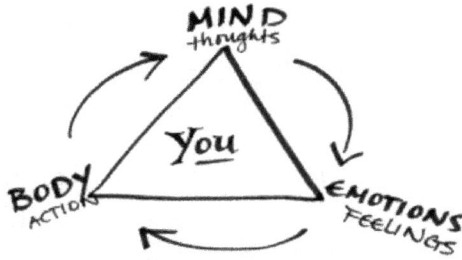

The Danger of Emotions

Executing a trade is not an emotional decision—it's an informed one. Your emotions can be your greatest enemy when it comes to trading. In order to trade successfully and profitably, your emotions must be under control and must be dealt with—not just pushed down and ignored.

Throughout the trading day there will be many news events about market activity that are intended to get your attention. You may find it tempting to react quickly to certain events, but you can't give in to this urge. You must always proceed with caution. Do exactly what you're supposed to do based on your trading plan (once you learn the technology of trading, you will have a plan for each trade, which includes rules for staying in and when to participate). Try not to let emotions alter your decisions too much. Sometimes this can be difficult to do, but when you've mastered this, you've truly overcome a major hurdle in your pathway to success. Many people don't realize it, but one of the most important aspects of success is a trader's self-control.

> *"A fool is quick tempered; the wise man stays cool in the face of insult or adversity."*
> **--Unknown**

Work Toward Continuous Self-Improvement

If you want to keep on succeeding, whether in life or business, you must be willing to continue to improve on what you know. Self-control, patience, discipline and a positive mental attitude are all excellent qualities. Having goals will help put those positive qualities into action and take you and your business to the next level. Physical activity also plays a part in achieving your goals. On the following pages, I'll explain why and then provide tips on goal setting.

Getting Physical

Have you ever thought that you would love to do something but you lack the energy? There's a pretty easy solution to this, and it's simply to get moving! There are all sorts of exercises you can do, depending on your personal health and physical capabilities. From chair yoga to simple stretches, resistance bands to running. It seems counterintuitive, but trust me—as long as you first consult with your doctor to get a medically approved plan, being active can help improve your mood and energy level. Note: I am not a doctor and this is not medical advice, it's merely a suggestion for improving your well-being. Always talk to your doctor before increasing your activity level or before starting an exercise plan.

Determining Your Goals

In life, whether it's in your career, your travels or your personal life, you need to have a sense of direction. Often, a list of goals fulfills that need—and this is especially true in trading. If you don't have trading goals, how do you expect to become a successful trader? Your trading goals can only be achieved through hard work and making sacrifices—but they can't be achieved at all if you don't set them. This approach applies to all goals you set for yourself, not just trading.

In trading, your goals are the individual steps that you must take in order to reach your dreams (i.e., to become a full-time professional trader). You must also be willing to consistently push yourself to attain these goals. Get excited about reaching the smaller goals, because a bunch of smaller goals eventually snowball into one or more of your bigger goals. Just realize that striving for excellence and success is a never-ending process, one that continues to evolve. Never stand still; always work to get better at what you do.

Tips for Setting Goals

Now you know that to be a successful trader, you must have goals. But you also have to learn how to set effective goals. Goal setting starts with an idea, a pad of paper, tablet or phone and you. Goals are created in three parts:

- **First** is creating the mental picture. You must be able to visualize your goal(s) and where your goal(s) will take you.
- **Second** is documentation. This brings reality to your vision. Writing your goals down can add clarity and dimension.

- **Third** is taking action toward achieving your goal(s). The best opportunities in life are the ones we create.

Goal setting provides you the opportunity to design a fulfilling life. If becoming a professional, full-time trader is your goal, there is absolutely no reason why you can't achieve that goal. In the following sections you will find step-by-step guides for achieving your personal and trading goals.

Tips for Achieving Your Personal Goals

- Write down your goals.
- Plan thoroughly.
- Be specific.
- Be decisive.
- Involve others (such as a mentor).
- Choose a realistic time frame.
- Stay focused.
- Maintain personal integrity.
- Take action.
- Expect changes.
- Reward yourself.

Tips for Achieving Your Trading Goals

- Write down your goals.
- Identify any obstacles and risks.
- Develop your trading plan.
- Identify any sacrifices and investments.
- List your personal benefits.

- Develop a support team (including role model(s)).
- Analyze your current situation.
- Determine the knowledge requirements.
- Set a deadline.
- Reward yourself now and then.

Understanding how to manage yourself and your time, how to control your opinions and bias, and how to make sure that you've prepared yourself effectively for your trading day is the true mark of a professional. You must act like a professional before you can call yourself one, so there's no better time than today to get started.

Chapter 3: Trading Basics

You wouldn't be reading this book if you didn't want to become a trader. But do you know what kind of trader you want to become? Not all traders are the same. There may be a specific type of trading that you're better suited for— but you'll never figure that out if you don't familiarize yourself with the four most common types of traders there are.

The Four Most Common Types of Traders

These four types of traders are all based on the typical length of time that you're in a trade. It boils down to which time frame (discussed shortly) that you will use for your trading decisions.

Scalpers

Scalpers are typically in and out of the markets several times during the day—as many as 30 to 40+ times during the day. They're only looking for very small moves and they never keep a trade overnight. Scalpers typically use small tick charts or one- to two-minute charts to make their trading decisions. You have to be a full-time trader to be able to trade like this.

Day Traders

Day traders are typically in and out of the markets one to five+ times a day, never keeping a trade overnight. Day traders typically use three-minute, five-minute, 15-minute and/or 30-minute charts to make their trading decisions. You should be able to devote a minimum of one to two hours during open market hours to become a day trader.

Swing Traders

Swing traders are not in and out during the trading day, but instead keep trades overnight. These types of trades can last anywhere from two days to a few weeks or longer, depending on what the market does. Swing traders typically use longer-term charts like daily or weekly charts to make their trading decisions.

Position Traders

Position traders hold a position for the long-term (from months to years). Position traders are not concerned with short-term fluctuations because they believe that their long-term investment horizons will smooth these out. Many position traders will take a look at weekly or monthly charts to get a sense of where the market is in a given trend. Position trading is the *polar opposite* of day trading because the goal is to profit from the move in the primary trend rather than the short-term fluctuations that occur day to day.

Trading Styles & Market Time Frames

Trading Style	Definition	Time Frame	Holding Period
Scalp trading	Many transactions per day held for very short time frames and traded based on small moves. This requires full-time attention and small time-frame charts. Trades are never kept overnight.	Very short-term	Seconds to minutes; no overnight positions
Day trading	Entering and exiting positions during the same trading day. All positions will usually be closed before market close.	Short-term	Day only; no overnight positions
Swing trading	Trades are held overnight from a couple of days to a few weeks.	Short-term	Days to weeks
Position trading	Positions are held for the long period. Short-term fluctuations are not an influence because the belief is that the long-term investment horizons will smooth them out.	Long-term	Months to years

Time Frames Used for Trading

There are different time frames used by different traders depending on the type of trader they are. This not only influences how long they hold positions but also which charts they use.

- **Weekly charts are used by longer-term position traders** to capture major trends in the markets. Each bar encompasses five trading days.
- **Daily charts are used by swing traders** to capture intermediate-term swings in an ongoing trend while sidestepping the brief countertrend (CT) moves. Each bar encompasses one full trading day.
- **Longer-term intraday and hourly intraday charts** (i.e., 240 minutes and 60 minutes) **are used by swing traders and day traders** to capture shorter-term swing trades that traders may hold overnight.
- **Intraday minute charts** (i.e., 30-, 15-, 5-, 3-, and/or 1-minute charts) **are used by day traders** for daily cash flow. Most day traders will use a 30-minute or 15-minute chart to help eliminate "noise" and to gain a clearer perspective of the shorter-term trend. Day traders will typically base their trade entries and exits off of five-minute or three-minute charts. Scalp traders will typically use the one-minute chart for really quick "scalp" trades. Either way, these shorter intraday time frames are used for trades that are not typically held overnight.

Fundamental Versus Technical Analysis

Trading decisions aren't just made based on how you feel—in fact, your emotions and feelings should almost never play a role in what you trade. Instead, you want to analyze data about the potential trade, which you can do through either fundamental or technical analysis.

Fundamental Analysis—Economics and News

With this method a trader attempts to study the reasons behind market movements, including macroeconomic factors within countries and industry conditions, and company-specific factors in the news (such as financial condition, value of shares in a company, profit and loss and management).

The purpose of fundamental analysis is to come up with an intrinsic value that an investor or trader can compare with the security's current price, with the goal of figuring out what sort of position to take with that security.

Technical Analysis—Chart Reading

Technical analysis is the study of the market action itself, primarily through the use of charts, for the purpose of forecasting price movement in order to make trading decisions. When using charts, trends and price patterns are identified.

The method you choose will depend on many factors but the truth is, no matter how you analyze the data, the market's movements are the only real truth there is. That's why technical analysis—which deals with the whats, not the whys—is going to be your best choice for making trading decisions.

Chapter 4: Going Deeper Into the World of Trading

Trading isn't just about buying in hopes of taking advantage and profiting from higher prices. First you need to learn how to read charts and get a feel for the market, but then you also need to learn how to sell the market short to try and profit from *lower* prices. Let's talk about that now since most people don't understand how to do that.

Selling Short

Smart traders have to be willing to sell short the market perhaps as often as they buy long the market (whenever it's necessary, of course—when the trend changes from up to down). As you know the markets do NOT go up all the time. A perfect example of this is from fall 2007 to spring 2009. In that time period we experienced one of the most agonizing bear markets in the last 70 years. Does the bear market from 2007 to 2009 mean that you couldn't make money during that time? Certainly not! In fact, you could have made a *lot* of money if you had known the correct strategies to use to short the market.

Common sense says to follow a market's overall trend (which you'll learn more about on page X). According to studies, only 2 percent of the American public ever shorts a market in their lifetime. A major reason for this is simply fear and ignorance. This is shocking when you understand that markets (and stocks) fall 67 percent to 80 percent faster than they rise. In other words, shorting stocks tends to compound money faster than buying a market to go long. Plus, if you're able to make money when the market is going down just as easily as when it goes up ... what is it that you have to be afraid of? Professional traders made billions from fall 2007 to spring 2009 by selling the markets short. The bottom line is that you must absolutely learn how to sell the markets short if you're ever going to be a successful trader. Fear and ignorance of selling short must be overcome.

Let's define what it means to sell short, or, to phrase it another way, "How do you sell a market you don't own?" To sell short stocks and ETFs, you simply borrow shares you don't own from your broker, order them sold and pocket the money. Then you wait for the price of the stock to drop. If it does, you buy the shares back at the lower price, turn them over to your broker (plus interest and commission) and keep the difference. It's that simple!

For the other trading instruments such as futures, commodities and foreign currencies, the concept of selling short is very similar. Futures, commodities and foreign currencies are traded via a performance bond so you only have to maintain the margin requirements in your account to trade them either long or short.

This is further proof that you absolutely need to be able to sell the market short. You would be missing out on 50 percent of the market moves if you didn't take advantage of bear markets.

Following is a weekly chart of the S&P 500 stock index showing how it dropped almost 800 points from fall 2007 until it hit bottom in spring 2009. There's an enormous amount of money to be made on a move like this!

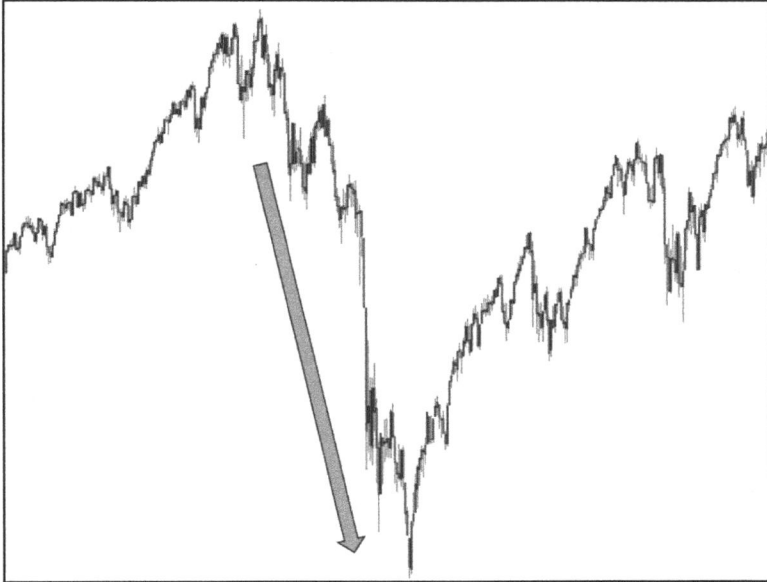

FIGURE 1: S&P 500 INDEX @ OPRA (WEEKLY BARS)

Why on earth would a trader be looking to *buy* stocks in a market like this as the markets continue to move lower?

Most investors (and uneducated traders) would be looking to buy this market as it moved lower because they are looking for a bargain ... but instead what they'll get is killed financially!

That's why you *must* learn to sell short the market.

Getting Technical

I want to start getting more technical now by showing you some basic approaches, or methodologies, to trading. To start, we need to discuss basic charts and trends. I'll then show market trends through chart examples with various time frames, ultimately illustrating why I believe price action is the single most important tool when trading.

Charts: I Have Some Explaining to Do

Two examples of charting that are used most frequently are *bar charts* and *candlestick charts*. Bar charts and candlestick charts show price movement or price action. They show the open, high, low and close of the price action over a given period of time (i.e., day, week, 60-minute, 30-minute, 15-minute, 5-minute, 3-minute, or 1-minute).

Bar Charts

As illustrated on the next page in Figure 2 and Figure 3, the top of the vertical line of a bar chart indicates the highest price that a market traded during the time period. The bottom represents the lowest price. The closing price is displayed on the right side of the bar and the opening price is shown on the left side of the bar. A single bar like those on the following page may represent one day, one week, 60 minutes, 15 minutes, or five minutes of trading.

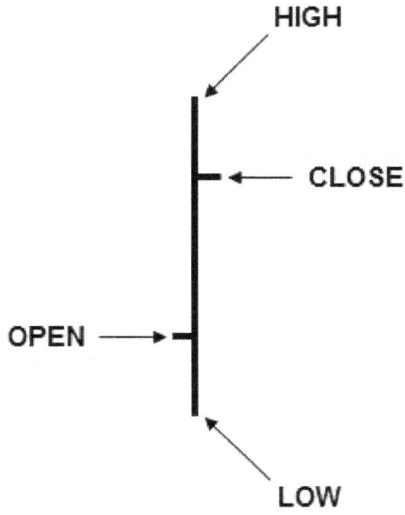

FIGURE 2: BULLISH PRICE BAR—HIGHER CLOSE

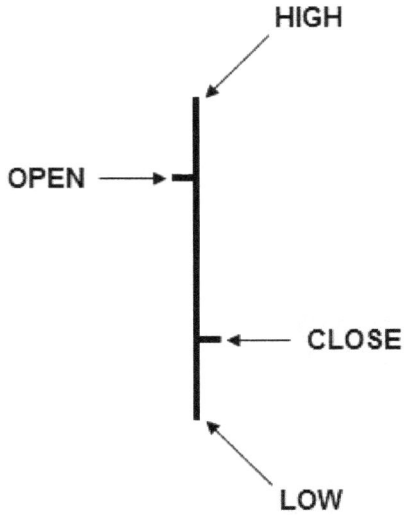

FIGURE 3: BEARISH PRICE BAR—LOWER CLOSE

FIGURE 4: QQQ: POWERSHARES QQQ TRUST, SERIES @
NASDAQ (DAILY BARS)

Candlestick Charts

Candlestick charts are commonly used by technical analysts. As illustrated below, the wide part of the candlestick is called the "real body" and tells traders whether the closing price was higher or lower than the opening price (white or green if the market closed higher, black or red if the market closed lower). The candlestick's shadows or "wicks" show the day's highs and lows and how they compare to the open and close. A single candlestick like the one on the next page may represent one day, one week, 60 minutes, 15 minutes, or five minutes of trading.

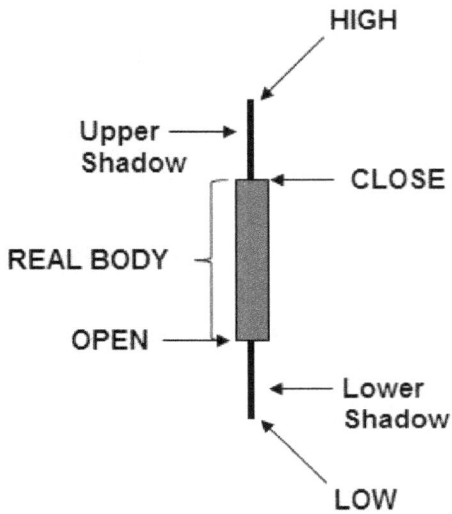

FIGURE 5: BULLISH CANDLESTICK
(HIGHER CLOSE)

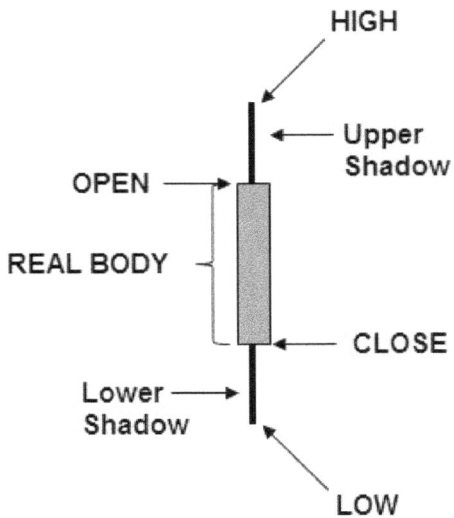

FIGURE 6: BEARISH CANDLESTICK
(LOWER CLOSE)

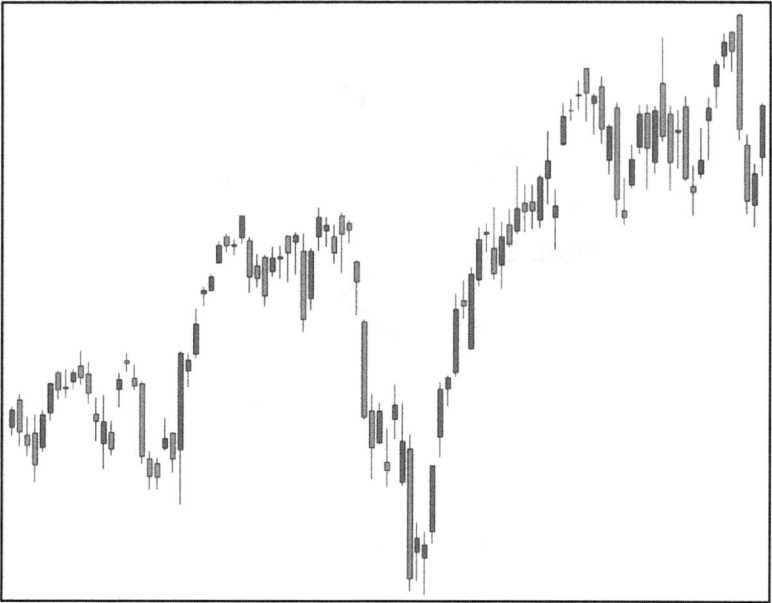

FIGURE 7: SPY: SPDR S&P 500 ETF TRUST @NYSE (DAILY BARS)

To create charts that work for your trading style, you need the right software. Here are some charting software providers I recommend:

- **TradeStation:** www.tradestation.com
- **NinjaTrader:** www.ninjatrader.com
- **Sierra Charts:** www.sierracharts.com
- **Trade Navigator:** www.genesisft.com
- **Stockcharts.com:** www.stockcharts.com
- **FreeStockCharts.com:** www.freestockcharts.com

Up and Down, Bull or Bear?

What is a trend these days? In basic terms, it's the general direction of trading for an overall market. A trend can be short-, intermediate- or long-term. Being able to identify a trend can help you grow your trading account if you are able to trade with the trend. As traders, we use charts to identify trends.

Trend Lingo

Here are a few common catchphrases or words used by traders to describe these two opposing forces (i.e., bull market and bear market).

Uptrend/Bull Market

A bull market is the time when buying is more dominant because prices are going up, or showing an uptrend. A bull market can also be discussed using the following terms:

- bullish
- buying long
- rally
- higher highs
- higher lows
- north
- trending up

Downtrend/Bear Market

A bear market is a general decline in the market over a period of time, showing a downtrend. Other terms used to reference a bear market include:

- bearish
- selling short
- selling off
- falling out of bed
- lower lows
- lower highs
- south
- trending down

Charts and Trading Trends Go Hand in Hand

You've just learned about bar charts, candlestick charts, bull markets and bear markets. What I want to do now is put a bunch of price bars together (i.e., regular bars or candlesticks) so that we're able to determine what the market is doing. This is the process traders use to make intelligent trading decisions. As you'll soon see, looking at a whole page of charts creates a picture that better informs your trading decisions.

What's Up With Charts?

Charts are visual representations of the price action of the markets (i.e., stocks, ETFs, options, stock index funds [E-Minis], forex currency pairs, bonds or commodities) over a given time period. We might think of charts as an artistic portrayal of the forces in the ongoing struggle for control between the bulls and bears. In reality, charts depict the ebb and flow of supply and demand in the marketplace.

I have always said, "A chart is a chart is a chart!" What I mean by that is, no matter what kind of chart you're looking at, it's going to give you a roadmap of the overall direction or trend of the market on either a short-, mid- or long-term basis. Charts reflect an *up*, *down* or *sideways* market. Identifying which wave/trend the market is in is critical to successful and profitable trading.

Uptrends

This is an example of an uptrend. The overall direction of the price movement is upward. This is indicated by a series of higher highs (peaks) and higher lows (troughs).

Downtrend

This is an example of a downtrend. The overall direction of the price movement is downward. You will see a series of progressively lower highs (peaks) and lower lows (troughs).

Sideways

This is an example of a sideways trend. The highs and lows are horizontal. In other words, the peaks and troughs are relatively equal or similar in appearance.

To recap, as you just learned, the market can only do one of three things: move up, down or sideways. You just have to know how to read the charts and know what to look for. The next two concepts, *support* and *resistance*, will show you when and where good low-risk, high-probability entries into the market are likely to take place.

Support and Resistance

One important aspect of reading a chart is knowing how to identify support and resistance levels. Support and resistance occur on all time frames and in all markets. Most traders understand what these levels are and use them in their trading. Therefore, these levels prove to be very reliable and predictable—kind of like a self-fulfilling prophecy. Understanding and using support and resistance will help ensure that you will trade on the same side as the professionals, which increases the accuracy of any trades you decide to place.

Support is a price level on a chart that rests under the current market price. When price has reached this general area, buying overwhelms the selling of a market. In other words, it's the point at which demand for a market exceeds supply. Support provides good buying opportunities. Support represents the lows or troughs of a sideways (also called *trading range*) market. See below:

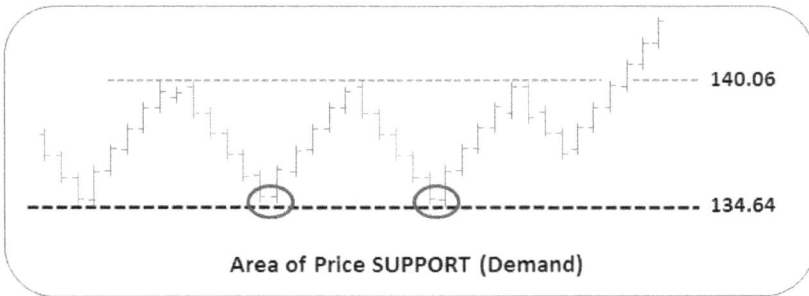

140.06

134.64

Area of Price SUPPORT (Demand)

Resistance is a price level on a chart that rests above the current market price. Resistance is the point at which selling overwhelms the buying of the market. In other words, it's where the supply for a market exceeds demand. Resistance provides good selling opportunities. Resistance is the highs or peaks of a sideways market. See below:

Area of Price RESISTANCE (Supply)

135.95

129.74

Resistance Becoming Support

In the figure below, when **resistance** was broken to the upside, it became **support**; thus **resistance becomes support** when broken to the upside.

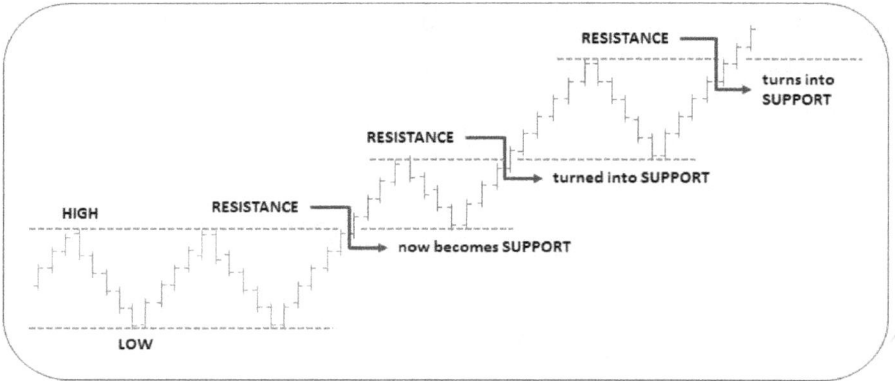

Support Becoming Resistance

In the figure below, when **support** was broken to the downside, it became **resistance**; thus **support becomes resistance** when broken to the downside.

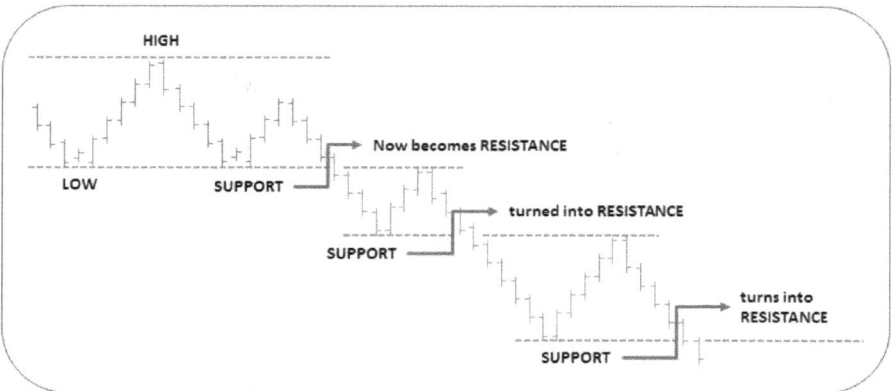

Sideways Market or Trading Range

On a chart, the movement of price within a well-defined pattern (i.e., relatively equal highs and equal lows) between support and resistance is called a trading range or *consolidation*. In general, this is where traders have agreed on what the price of a market should be. Periods of consolidation are found on charts in all time frames and in all markets.

SIDEWAYS MARKET
(consolidation)

SIDEWAYS MARKET
(consolidation)

In a trading range (consolidation), once the price of a market breaks through support or resistance, you will typically see volatility increase, creating a potential opportunity for traders to enter the market and potentially generate a profit.

The point of knowing all this information about charts and how to interpret them is so that you can make the most informed trading decisions possible based on the market's actual *price action*. Let's talk about this concept in more detail.

What Is Price Action?

Price action is simply price movement. Price action is a reflection of what traders think a market is worth and is illustrated on price charts. Candlestick charts and bar charts are necessary for analyzing price action because they help traders visualize price movement.

If you take one thing away from reading this book, let it be that *price action is king*!

I like to emphasize the importance of price action in making your trading decisions. Tuning in to price action means tuning out of Wall Street media hype. Instead, learn to use and concentrate on price action. The key is to chart your course and stay focused on your goal. The goal is to learn how to read price action like a daily newspaper, regardless of the financial instrument you decide to trade.

At the end of the day, it really doesn't matter what's happening with the economy, the industry or any other external factor. Everything you absolutely need to know about a market is reflected on its price chart. Markets are driven by human emotions, namely fear and greed. Therefore, it is our responsibility to understand how to read a price chart to understand whether fear or greed is the primary driver at the moment, and to use that information in order to trade a market profitably.

Let's look at some key phrases and truths about price action. Reading these should help you understand exactly how important price action is to your overall success as a trader. Please read and learn them as if your financial future depends on it—because it does!

> *"You don't get any profit from fundamental analysis. You get profit from buying and selling. So why stick with the appearance when you can go right to the reality of PRICE."*
> **- Legendary trader Richard Dennis**

- Price action must always come first.
- Price is never wrong. The market (price) is right 100 percent of the time.
- Price is the only reality and truth in the market.
- The only indicator available to us that doesn't lag is price.
- All technical indicators are derived from price (i.e., open, high, low and close), so why not go straight to the source: price.
- All successful traders know how to read and interpret price.
- Pure price action of any market knows more than any Wall Street analyst or economist.
- Good traders don't have to know what's fundamentally going on inside of a market. A chart is a chart is a chart—period.
- Price is everything and areas where price has turned in the past are likely to be areas where it will turn again.
- Price is reality. Intelligence is the appearance. As traders, we are trading mob psychology. We're

trading numbers reflected on a price chart and that's all we're doing.

Now, let's go through some commonly used tools that many traders use to help predict what the market is likely going to do next.

Moving Averages and Indicators

Although we typically focus on price action, beginner traders can use moving averages and indicators to help them interpret charts. The two most common moving averages are the simple moving average and the exponential moving average. After we discuss these two moving averages, we'll then move into the three most common indicators used today.

Simple Moving Average

The simple moving average (SMA) is a moving average calculated by adding up the closing prices of a market for a number of time periods (i.e., 20 days) and dividing that total by the same number of time periods (20). For example, a 20-period simple moving average would be calculated by adding up the last 20 closing prices for whatever time frame chart you are using and dividing that total by 20. This shows us the average price of a market over a certain period of time (i.e., 20 days).

Exponential Moving Average

The exponential moving average (EMA) is similar to the simple moving average except that more weight is given to the latest closing prices. An exponential moving average reacts faster to recent price changes than a simple moving average.

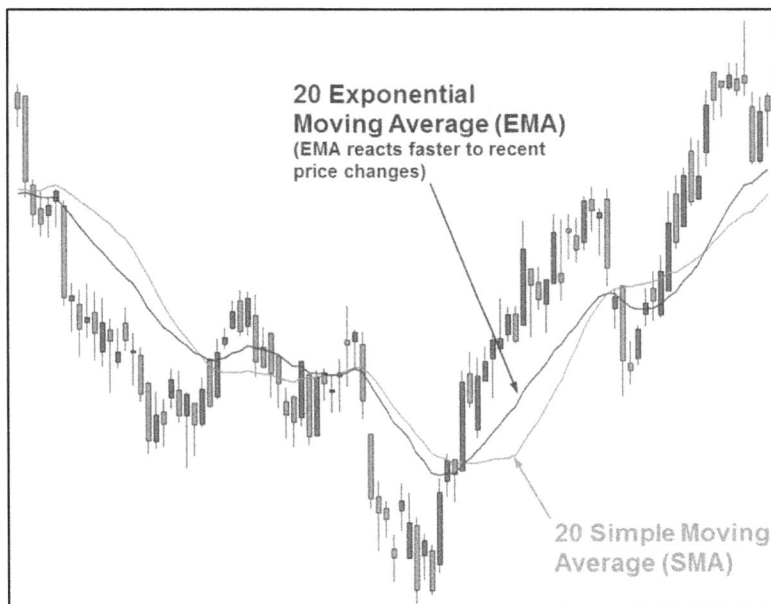

FIGURE 8: OIH: OILS SERVICES HOLDRS @ NYSE (DAILY BARS)

Key Moving Average Concepts to Understand

Rising moving averages (MAs) generally represent positive market action or strength. Declining MAs generally represent negative market action or weakness.

The sharper the slopes of the MAs, the stronger the market is in that direction. This important concept applies to both **upward** and **downward** slopes.

During strong **uptrends,** pullbacks tend to halt at/near rising MAs and offer **good buying opportunities.** During strong **downtrends**, rallies tend to halt at/near declining MAs **offering good selling opportunities.**

An **upward penetration** through (or break through) a **rising MA** is considered **bullish**; therefore, good **buy** opportunities present themselves when a strong market pulls back down to/near its rising MAs and holds.

A **downward penetration** through a **declining MA** is considered **bearish**; therefore, good **sell** opportunities present themselves when a weak market pulls back up to/near its declining MAs and holds.

There have been many successful trading systems built around a moving average crossover signal. For example, in the chart on the next page, traders will look to:

- *Buy* on a pullback into a logical support area when a nine-period EMA crosses above a 21-period EMA, and/or
- *Sell* on a pullback into a logical resistance when a nine-period EMA crosses below a 21-period EMA.

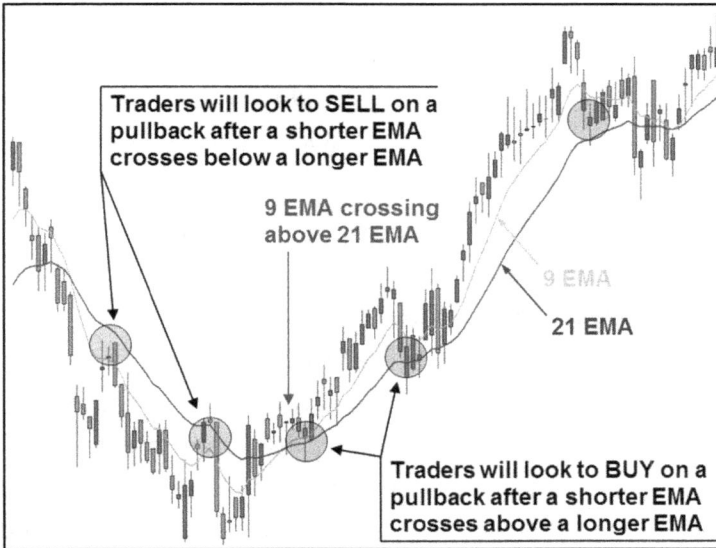

So there you have it—a brief discussion of the two most commonly used moving averages (i.e., SMA and EMA). As you can see in the chart on the previous page, they can be very powerful tools for identifying the trend and giving potential trading opportunities when used correctly.

What Is a Technical Indicator?

In the context of technical analysis, an indicator is a mathematical calculation based on a price and/or volume. The result is used to predict future prices. Common technical indicators are:

- **Moving Average Convergence-Divergence (MACD):** MACD is a very effective momentum indicator. The MACD turns two trend-following indicators (moving averages) into a momentum oscillator. As a result, the MACD offers the best of both worlds: trend following and momentum. The MACD fluctuates above and below the zero line as the moving averages converge, cross and diverge. The MACD indicator has enough strength to be used on its own, but its predictive function is not absolute. Used with another indicator, the MACD can really increase the trader's advantage.

- **Relative Strength Index (RSI):** RSI is an extremely popular momentum oscillator that measures the speed and change of price movements. RSI oscillates between zero and 100. Traditionally, RSI is considered overbought when above 70 and oversold when below 30.

- **Stochastics:** Stochastics is a momentum indicator that shows the location of the close relative to the high-low range over a fixed number of periods. Stochastics follows the speed or the momentum of price. As a rule, the momentum changes direction before price; therefore, bullish and bearish divergences in the Stochastics can be used to foreshadow reversals. Because Stochastics is range bound, it is also useful for identifying overbought and oversold levels.

Moving Average Convergence-Divergence

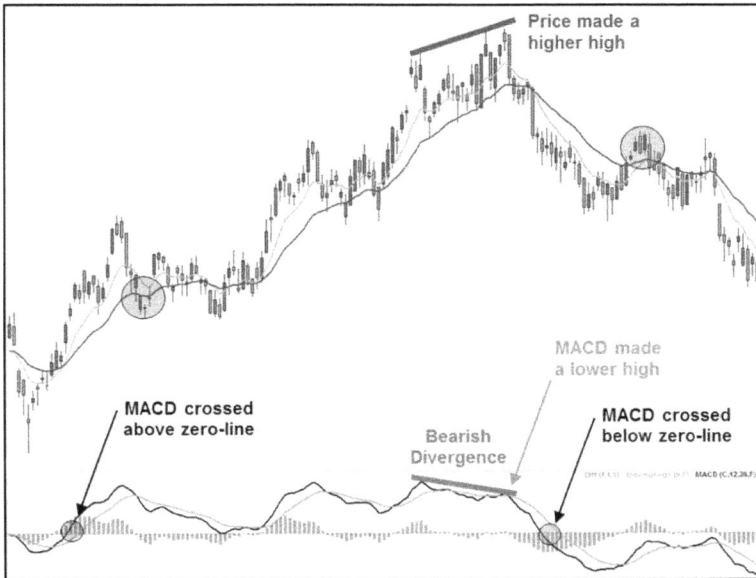

Traders can look for signal line crossovers, centerline crossovers and divergences in moving average convergence-divergence (MACD) and price to generate signals. As you can see in the chart above:

- Once the **MACD crossed and held above the zero-line,** a pullback into logical support offered a great buying opportunity.
- The longer an uptrend continues with higher highs and higher lows, the more likely a market is to turn and potentially reverse. **Bearish divergence** (price made higher highs while MACD failed and made a lower high) in the MACD provided clues to the upcoming reversal.

63

- Once the **MACD crossed and held below the zero-line,** a pullback into logical resistance offered a great selling opportunity.

Relative Strength Index

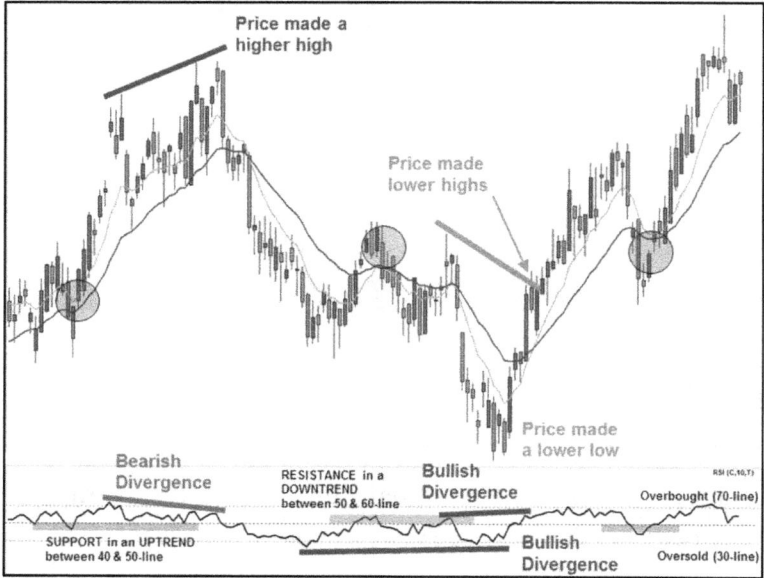

Traders look for divergences in relative strength index (RSI) and price, failure swings and centerline crossovers. RSI can also be used to identify the general trend identification.

- In an uptrend, RSI tends to fluctuate between 40 and 90 with the 40- to 50-line acting as support (buying opportunities). Conversely, in a downtrend, RSI tends to fluctuate between 60 and 10 with the 50- to 60-line acting as resistance (selling opportunities).

- The longer a trend continues, the more likely a market is to potentially reverse. Bearish divergence (price makes higher highs while RSI fails and makes a lower high below 70-line) in the RSI provides clues of a potential reversal to the downside. Conversely, bullish divergence (price makes lower lows while RSI fails and makes higher lows above 30-line) in the RSI provides clues of a potential reversal to the upside.

- Double bullish divergence (very strong bullish signal) is identified on the chart on the previous page in the RSI when, at the beginning of February 2014, the RSI made higher highs and lows while the price action made lower lows and lower highs.

Stochastics

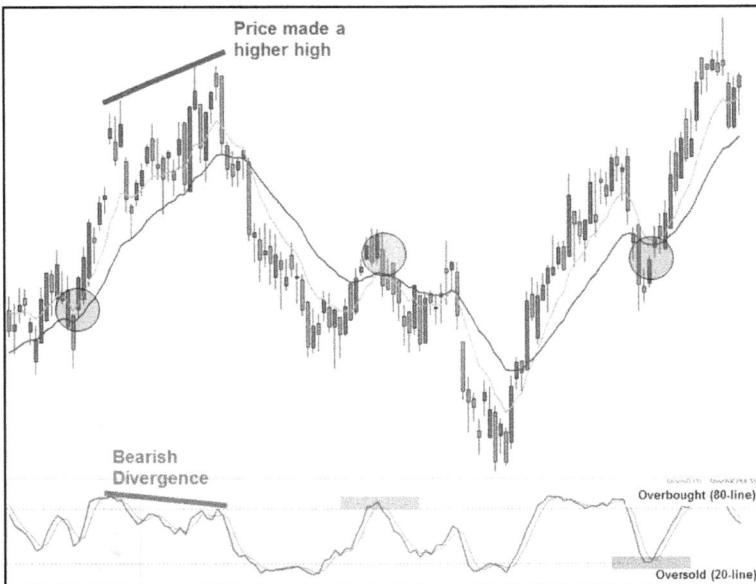

Traders look for divergences in Stochastics and price to identify overbought and oversold levels.

- The longer an uptrend continues with higher highs and higher lows, the more likely a market is to turn and potentially reverse. **Bearish divergence** (price made higher highs while Stochastics failed and made a lower high below 80-line) in Stochastics provides clues of a potential reversal to the downside.

- In a downtrend, the market typically becomes oversold when Stochastics declines below 20 (buying opportunities if the market is trading at support). Conversely, in an uptrend, the market typically becomes overbought when Stochastics rises above 80 (selling opportunities if the market is trading at resistance).

What Is Volatility?

Most traders refer to volatility as the speed with which the price of a market rises and falls within a given time period. You can see the volatility of a market just by looking at its chart:

- A market's price in a higher volatility setting will change dramatically over a short period of time and the range (from high to low) of the price bars or

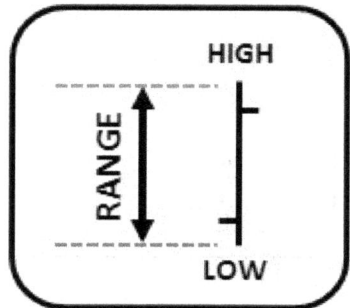

candlesticks on a chart will be higher than normal.

- A market's price in a lower volatility setting does not fluctuate dramatically over a short period of time, but changes at a steady pace. The range (from high to low) of the price bars or candlesticks on a lower volatility market will be lower than normal.

It's easy enough to look at the values on the right of a chart and determine whether you are looking at a volatile or a nonvolatile market. However, a trader can identify volatility by looking at the range or average true range (ATR) of a market.

Range is directly proportional to volatility. Range is defined as the change of value in price per increment of time, or simply the difference between a market's high price and low price for a particular time frame.

The average true range (ATR) is an indicator available in most charting software that measures volatility by defining the average range of price bars and candlesticks along with capturing volatility from an overnight gap up or down.

Market volatility is inevitable. It's the nature of the markets to move up and down over the short-term. You need to understand the basics of volatility and how to measure it because it <u>will</u> influence how you trade. **Everything from your entries, your stops, your profit objectives and your position size will all be greatly influenced by the volatility of the markets you're trading.**

A General Rule of Thumb

When a market is trending up, the market tends to be a lot less volatile than when a market is trending down. Therefore, generally speaking, a downtrending market is much more volatile than an uptrending market. A market falls roughly three times more quickly than it rises.

Chapter 5: Creating Yourself as a Trader

There are many different choices to make when you start your trading career. It's not just about deciding how much money to set aside for trading, it's also about determining the trading style you're most suited for and coming up with a money management plan.

Common Trading Styles

- Breakout trading
- Retracement and/or pullback trading
- Trend trading
- Countertrend trading

Breakout Trading

Breakout trading can be defined in two ways:

1. When you look to buy the market as the market is making higher highs or when you look to sell the market as the market is making lower lows.

2. When you look to buy the market above the high of a trading range or sell the market below the low of a trading range. In this particular scenario, you don't care which way the market moves. However, you do know that when the market breaks in one direction (i.e., above the **highs** or below the **lows**), you'll be

69

there to take advantage of the price move (either up
or down).

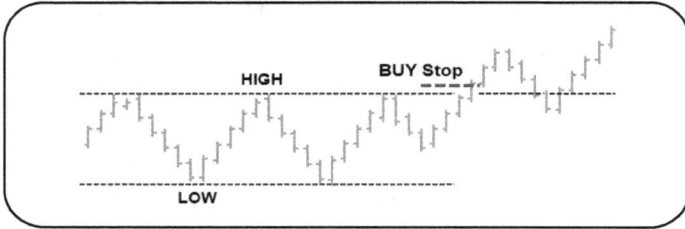

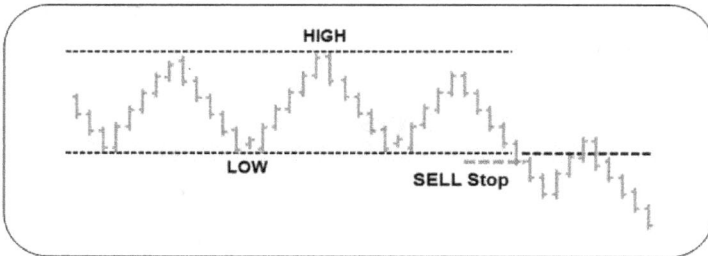

Retracement and/or Pullback Trading

Retracement and/or *pullback trading* is when you look for an
established trend to develop and simply wait for a
retracement or pullback before getting into the market in
that trend direction.

For example, if the trend were up, you would simply wait
for the market to pull down off a new high (NH) into a
logical place of support before buying the market (traders
use the term "entering long" when referring to buying).

Conversely, if the trend were down, you simply would wait for the market to pull up off a new low (NL) into a logical place of resistance before selling the market (traders use the term "entering short" when referring to selling).

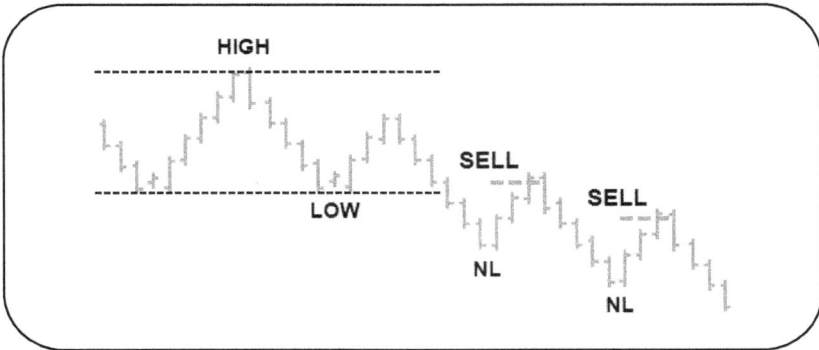

Trend Trading

Trend trading is simply trading *with* the current trend in an attempt to make consistent profits in the direction of the prevailing trend, and occasionally, catch most of the trend.

71

Countertrend Trading

Countertrend trading is simply trading *against* the current trend in the attempt to profit from a potential reversal. For example, a trader who is assuming a downtrend may be reversing to the upside will take on a bullish position (buy or go long) when the prices are low. A trader who is assuming an uptrend may be reversing to the downside will take on a bearish position (sell or go short) when the prices are high.

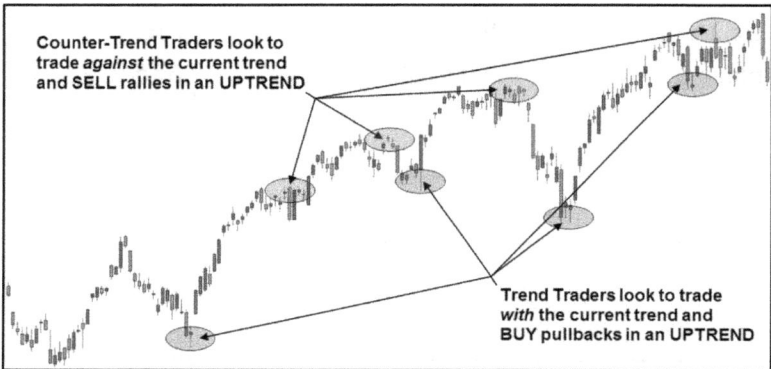

Trend Trading vs. Countertrend Trading

Most beginner traders try to catch tops and bottoms in the market and do not even try to trade *with* the trend. When I first started trading, like many other new traders, I attempted to do the same thing. So, I know not only from my own personal experience but also from teaching and talking to tens of thousands of traders that many traders tend to do the same thing.

Many (if not most) traders feel that trying to catch a market top or bottom is where the real money is. My experience, and that of my students, has taught me differently. Catching directional moves *with* the trend adds up and is easier to do than trying to catch a top or bottom in the market. Occasionally, you will catch the beginning of a new trend and take advantage of most of the trend.

I strongly suggest concentrating mostly on trend trades in the beginning as opposed to trying to pick tops and bottoms. Your winning percentages will be much higher when you're trading in the direction of the trend and it will be much easier for you to make money. I'll go as far as to say you probably won't become a successful trader by trying to pick tops and bottoms when you first start off trading. Countertrend (CT) trading takes a lot more experience. Believe me when I say that you'll find trading less stressful and much more rewarding and profitable if you simply stick to trading with a market's overall trend.

Managing Your Money

Wise money management is the basis of any good trading methodology and is what will ultimately help distinguish a consistently successful trader from the trader who consistently loses. What I would like to discuss now is the administrative side of your trading plan.

Money management addresses the question of how best to use the capital available to you in the most effective manner possible with the goal of maximizing your profitability while at the same time protecting your capital by minimizing the risk of ruin.

The True Essence of Money Management Is Managing Risk

Many traders have fallen to the wayside trying to make a lot of money on a single trade. Trying to hit that "home run" when they would have been better off making small (singles and doubles), steady gains. Once you start doing this and thinking this way, you will see your account start to consistently grow.

Money management includes consideration of the following factors:

- Deciding on the optimum amount of money to commit to any one trade relative to your total available trading capital.
- Protecting your profits from erosion.
- Avoiding (at all costs) turning a small losing trade into a huge losing trade. If you keep your losses small, your profits don't have to be "home runs" to earn a good living.
- Knowing when and how to increase the size of your cash commitment when the odds are more in your favor (i.e., risk to reward is really tilted in your favor, etc.).
- Recognizing the importance of taking some of your winnings off the table after a winning streak.
- Knowing your exit before you enter. One of the cardinal rules of good trading is to always have an exit point before you even enter a trade.
- Knowing your initial risk so that you can express all your results in terms of your initial risk.

Managing Risk with Stop Losses

We have no control over or influence over the market's behavior. But that doesn't mean we have to leave ourselves exposed to the threat of a suddenly shifting trend or unexpected change in the direction of a market. A stop loss is a method of gaining *some control over your trades.* A stop loss is the level at which you will close a trade on the basis that it has gone too far in the wrong direction and therefore no longer gives reason for being in that trade. <u>Always</u> use a stop loss when trading. It's too common that a small loss becomes a larger loss if you do not draw that line in the sand and exit the market when you realize you are wrong about your analysis. A consistently profitable trader will take a small loss and go on to the next trade.

In trading, you'll always be taking on some risk, but as long as you take the money management guidelines I've provided into account and learn where to place your stops, you'll be able to trade without such a fear factor. **I recommend that you never risk more than 2 percent of your entire account on any one trade.** I would even go as far as to say not to risk more than 1 percent of your account when first starting off until you feel comfortable and have consistent results. Until then I recommend paper or simulated trading before committing any real money.

Chapter 6: Becoming the Trader You Want to Be

If you're not going to do your best at something, there's really no point in doing it at all. In this chapter, I want to focus on ways you can recreate yourself as a successful, confident, consistently profitable trader. To do so, I'm going to share some rules, some last-minute words of wisdom, and ask you some questions about the type of trader you want to be.

Twenty Rules for Trading Success

- **Always use stops.** Risk control is the true measure of a good, consistent trader. If you lose all your capital on the lemons, you can't play when the great trades set up. Consider cash as having an option value.
- **Don't overtrade.** This is the number-one reason why individual traders and investors lose money. Look at your trades from the past year and apply the 90/10 rule. Dump the least profitable 90 percent and watch your performance skyrocket. Then aim for that most profitable 10 percent of trades. Overtrading is a great early retirement plan for your broker, not you.
- **Don't forget to sell.** Date your positions—don't marry them. Remember, pigs get slaughtered.

Always leave the last 10-15 percent of a move for the next guy.

- **Don't chase the market.** If you do, it will turn back and bite you. Wait for it to come to you. If you miss the train, there will be another one along in hours, days, weeks or months. Patience is truly a profitable virtue in this business.

- **When you put on a position, calculate how much you are willing to lose to keep it.** Then put a stop just below there. If it gets triggered, you'll just walk away. Only enter a trade when the risk/reward is in your favor. You can start at 2:1. That means only risk a dollar to potentially make two.

- **Always be willing to go long (buy) and short (sell).** You have to be flexible and dynamic in your trading. One minute a trader could be long the market and the very next minute they may be short the market. You need to be able to flip-flop, to be quick and nimble in your trading.

- **Don't think you have to be a genius to play this game.** If that were required, Wall Street would have run out of players a long time ago. If you employ risk control and stops, then you can be wrong 40 percent of the time and still make a living. That's a little better than a coin toss. If you're wrong only 30 percent of the time, you can make millions. If you're wrong only 20 percent of the time, you're heading a trading desk at Goldman Sachs. If you're wrong a mere 10 percent of the time, you're running a $20 billion hedge fund that the public only hears about when you pay/invest $100 million. And if someone tells you they're never wrong, as is often claimed on the internet, run away because it's simply impossible!

- **Be prepared to work hard.** Trading attracts a lot of wide-eyed, naïve but lazy people because it appears so easy from the outside. You buy a stock (futures contract, forex, option, ETF, etc.), watch it go up and make money. How hard is that? The reality is that successful trading and/or investing is hard work, often requiring twice as much work as a normal job. The more research you put into a trade, the more comfortable you will become and the more profitable it will be.

- **Don't confuse a bull market with brilliance.** When the market goes straight up (i.e., 1995 to 2000), anybody can make money.

- **Don't believe the media.** Look for the hard data, the numbers, and you'll see that often the talking heads, the paid industry apologists and politicians don't know what they're talking about.

- **Remember that sometimes the conventional wisdom is right.**

- **Invest like a fundamentalist, execute like a technical analyst.** Trade using technical analysis, then gain an understanding of basic fundamentals. This will make you an even better trader.

- **Learn how to read charts like a daily newspaper. This is key to successful trading.** That said, you

79

should also learn what an "outside vertical bar" is and who the hell Leonardo Fibonacci is.

- **The simpler a market approach, the better it works (the "KISS" method).** Everyone talks about buying low and selling high, but few actually do it. All black boxes eventually blow up, if they were ever there in the first place.

- **Remember that markets are made up of people.** Understand and anticipate how traders think and you will make a lot of money. The market is made up of people's fear and greed. It's all psychological. Learn how to read people and you'll certainly be ahead of everybody else.

- **Understand what information is in the market and what isn't and you will make more money.**

- **Do the hard trade, the one that everyone tells you is crazy.** If you add a position and then throw up or feel sick afterwards, then you know you've done the right thing.

- **If you are trying to get out of a hole, the first thing to do is quit digging and throw away the shovel—exit your trade ASAP.** A blank/neutral/flat position can be invigorating.

- **Making money in the market is an unnatural act.** Humans are predators and hunters, evolved to track game on the horizon of an African savanna. Modern humans are maybe five million years old, but civilization has been around for only 10,000 years. Our brains have not had time to make the adjustment to looking past the surface logic of a market's actions into the underlying reasons behind the movement. This means that if a stock has gone up, your brain believes it will continue to go up. To make money, you have to go against these innate instincts. Some people are born with this ability, while others can only learn it through years of training.

One final bit of advice: remember what John Maynard Keynes, the great economist and early hedge fund trader of the thirties, once said: "Markets can remain illogical longer than you can remain solvent." Hang around long enough, and you will see this proven time and time again.

Twenty Truisms Applicable to Trading

Next, I wanted to share 20 smart sentiments that I think are very applicable to your life in general and can apply to your trading. My true intention here is not only to help you become a better trader but also to help you become a better person in general.

- Be faithful and *honest* with yourself in your trading; be diligent and consistent and it will bring you prosperity.
- Those who *work their plan will prosper,* but those who chase fantasies lack judgment.
- *Steady plodding* brings *prosperity;* hasty speculation brings poverty.

- Those who want to *do right* will get a *rich reward*, but those who want to get rich quick will quickly fail.
- Trying to *get rich quick* is wrong and leads to poverty.
- Wealth taken from gambling quickly disappears; wealth from diligent effort and hard work grows.
- *Follow the rules* and keep your financial life intact; ignoring the rules means financial ruin.
- A person without self-control is as defenseless as a city with broken-down walls.
- The wise control their temper. They know that anger causes mistakes.
- The intelligent are always open to new ideas; in fact, they look for them.
- *Get all the advice that you can* and be wise all the rest of your life.
- Fools despise advice; the wise consider each suggestion.
- Fools think they need no advice but the wise listen to others.
- To learn, you must want to be taught. To refuse correction is stupid.
- Anyone willing to be corrected is on the path to success. Those who refuse correction have lost their chance.
- *Hard work brings prosperity;* playing around brings poverty.
- If you love sleep, you will end up in poverty. Stay awake, work hard, and there will be plenty to eat.

- The foolish will lose in the end; the wise will end with the winnings.
- The wise save up for the future, but the foolish spend whatever they get.
- Truth *stands the test of time;* lies are soon exposed.

Final Review

Before I get into the self-assessment to help you design yourself as a trader, I want to briefly review the various financial instruments from which we all can profit and the types of traders that exist based on length of trades.

The financial instruments from which we all can profit are:

- Stocks
- ETFs
- Options
- Stock index futures (E-Minis)
- Bonds
- Commodities
- Forex currency pairs

Now, ask yourself these simple questions:

- What financial instrument(s) do I want to trade?
- Why am I interested in trading this/these instrument(s)?
- Do I have any biases or attraction impacting my decision?
- Does it really matter which market I trade?

Only you can answer these questions; there are no right or wrong answers. In my own personal opinion, each of the markets listed can be traded on a very similar basis. As long as you can chart it, you can trade it profitably—if you know what you're doing. As I mentioned earlier in the book, a chart is a chart is a chart; if it can be charted and there is enough liquidity and volatility, I will trade it when the trade setups occur. The one exception is trading options; you really need to understand how they work and what strategies best fit the current market conditions. Of course, you will want to use the trading strategies that gel with you personally.

Next you need to consider your preferred trading time frame. The time frames that best suit you, in terms of your personality, temperament and time commitments are even more important than the financial instrument(s) you ultimately decide to trade. Everything that I teach you can be applied to any market and any time frame.

Let's take a look again at the four most common types of traders based on length of time they're in a trade.

Scalper: These types of traders are typically in and out of the markets several times during the day—some as many as 30 to 40+ times during the day. They're only looking for very small moves and they never keep a trade overnight. Scalpers typically use small tick charts or one- to two-minute charts to make their trading decisions. You have to be a *full-time* trader to be able to trade like this.

Day trader: These types of traders are typically in and out of the markets one to five+ times a day, never keeping a trade overnight. Day traders typically use three-minute, five-minute, 15-minute and/or 30-minute charts to make their trading decisions. You should be able to *devote a minimum of one to two hours during the 9:30 a.m. ET to 4:00 p.m. ET trading session* to become a day trader.

Swing trader: These types of traders are not in and out during the trading day, but rather they keep trades overnight. These types of trades can last anywhere from 2 days to a few weeks or longer, depending on what the market does. Swing traders typically use longer-term intraday charts or daily charts to make their trading decisions. You only need to devote roughly 20 to 30 minutes a day to this type of trading.

Position trader: This type of trader holds a position for the long-term (from months to years). Position traders are not concerned with short-term fluctuations because they believe that their long-term investment horizons will smooth these out. Many position traders will take a look at weekly or monthly charts to get a sense of where the market is in a given trend. Position trading is the polar opposite of day trading because the goal is to profit from the move in the primary trend rather than the short-term fluctuations that occur day to day.

This also goes for exiting with a profit using logical profit objectives or for deciding whether to use a trailing stop; the market will dictate when you exit the market, based on how long it takes to reach these price levels. Therefore, you cannot possibly know with any certainty how long you will actually be in a trade. Remember, it's all about the length of time that you're in a trade. Position traders typically use weekly and monthly charts, but they also use daily charts for their trade setups too (just like swing traders). You only need to *devote roughly about 10 to 15 minutes a day*, if that, to this type of trading.

Once you learn how to enter, exit and manage a trade, you're going to let the market dictate how long you're in a trade. The market is either going to keep you in for a longer time because it's moving favorably in your trade direction, or the market will stop you out for a relatively quick and small loss.

One other thing that is very important for you to understand: *trading is fractal*. That means the same trading methods I mentioned earlier apply to *all* markets and *all* time frames; they are universal in nature. You will not be limited to trading only one type of financial instrument, either. If you can chart it, you can trade it profitably; this always has been my motto.

What Type of Trader Will You Be?

The <u>YOU</u> Assessment: Questions for Maximizing Your Trading Potential

Given that 70 to 80 percent of trading is emotional and psychological, you truly need to understand yourself to succeed. In order to understand yourself, you need to go through a brief trader (<u>YOU</u>) assessment. There are six components that I believe make every trader unique. Once you've identified what these are for you, you will have a better understanding of what markets you should be trading and what time frames are best suited to you and your personality. Answering these questions as honestly as possible will help point you in the right direction, which ultimately will help make you a better and more successful trader.

The six components that you need to delve into, which I like to call "**YOU** Questions for Maximizing Your Potential," are as follows:

1. YOUR personality
2. YOUR comfort level
3. YOUR time commitment
4. YOUR energy level
5. YOUR capital commitment
6. YOUR wants, needs and desires (what YOU want to achieve from your trading or investing)

Believe it or not, many traders don't give these questions a second thought, yet they are so, so important. Think about it—how you trade, what you trade and the frequency of the trades you make all come down to who you are as a person, and not what you know about a specific financial instrument.

In delving a bit deeper into each of these factors, you will start to understand exactly what I mean with more clarity. You'll start to identify the various aspects of your unique personality, comfort level, time commitment, energy level, capital commitment and specific wants, needs and desires, which will help clarify your vision of yourself as a trader. You are as unique as your fingerprints; nobody else's fingerprints are the same as yours. That is why you must figure out what financial instruments and time frames best suit YOU.

Let me give you a few examples of what I'm talking about:

(1) There are traders who are great at trading options and make money consistently, but who can't make any money when they try to day trade stocks.

(2) There are other traders who are fantastic day traders, but who can't trade options profitably.

(3) There are those traders who prefer to day trade futures and/or foreign currencies, yet have no desire to hold positions overnight; their stomachs can't handle it and they have no patience for this type of trading.

(4) Finally, there are traders who simply want to swing trade stocks, ETFs and/or options on stocks or ETFs, all with the goal of looking to supplement their incomes safely, conservatively and consistently, or to grow their retirement accounts.

I could give you tons of other examples, but I think you get the picture. By reading these examples, I hope you're starting to see the importance of really understanding what type of trading is best suited for you. I think you'll agree that you don't want to trade the wrong markets and wrong time frames and lose money as a result, all because you didn't think this through thoroughly.

Each person has an area of trading that fits them personally. I highly doubt you want to be in one of those areas that doesn't work for you simply because you didn't give this enough thought.

Trading is no different from any other worthwhile, high-performance occupation; to be truly exceptional at something, you must first have the passion and drive to succeed. This is especially important for trading. You also need to completely immerse yourself in your profession. Becoming a professional trader is absolutely no different from becoming an accountant, lawyer, engineer or doctor. It takes a tremendous amount of commitment, discipline, patience and a strong desire to succeed.

I believe it all starts here, with you asking yourself the **<u>YOU</u> Questions for Maximizing Your Potential.** Remember, *how you trade*, *what you trade* and the *frequency of your trades* all come down to **who you are as a person**. It's not about what you know about a specific financial instrument or time frame you ultimately use for your trading.

By simply reading through this section, you're probably getting a better understanding of exactly where you are and where you probably should be, and we haven't even gone through the <u>YOU</u> questions yet. Let's get to it.

When you read, think about and start answering the questions, think about everything that I've mentioned up to this point (i.e., various financial markets and length of trades); then, gradually start placing yourself in the category of the type of trader who makes the most sense to you. Remember, there are no right or wrong answers here. This is simply aimed at helping you learn exactly what type of trading is best suited to you. Only you will know this—no one else will, so really think about each question and place yourself where you think you ought to be as a trader.

You'll notice that a number of these questions are geared toward those who already trade. For some of these questions, you will understand them better once you start trading. You can easily come back to answer those questions after you have started trading.

Section 1: Questions About Your Personality

These questions are meant to dig deeper to see if you tend to follow rules, how you learn the best and many other aspects of how you feel about the markets. Remember, there are no right or wrong answers; these questions (and your answers) are for **you** only.

- Do you fail to place a protective stop because you don't want to take an actual loss?
- Do you have the right beliefs and attitude for successful trading?
- Do you believe that your trading plan will make money over the long run? Remember, you are what you believe.

- Do you typically trade against the market direction (picking tops and bottoms versus trading with the trend)? People often need to always be right—not a good quality in anyone, especially traders.
- Do you often trade with no plan of action?
- Do you like to follow instructions?
- When you buy something that has to be put together, do you read the instructions first or do you attempt to put it together without reading the instructions?
- Are you a quick learner?
- How do you best learn?
    - **Visual learners**: Usually, but not always, scalpers and/or day traders.
    - **Auditory learners**: Usually, but not always, day traders and/or shorter-term swing traders.
    - **Kinesthetic learners**: Many times, but not always, swing/position traders.

Section 2: Questions About Your Comfort Level

Your answers to these questions can indicate a few things—namely, what your comfort level is when trading the markets.

- When the market closes each day, do you feel happy or exhausted (i.e., set reasonable goals; less is more)?
- Do you typically feel stressed when you trade?
- Do you think most of your stress is self-induced?

- o If you have a **low comfort level**, that usually means you feel a lot of pressure when trading.
- o If you have a **medium comfort level**, you typically feel a moderate amount of pressure when trading.
- o If you have a **high risk tolerance (comfort level)**, you typically will feel very little pressure when you trade, which can be a very good thing.
- Can you sleep at night with a position on?
- Do you get really nervous right after an entry? Shooting for home run trades = stress; small positions are easier to hold and they make it easier to follow your trading plan.
- Do you come to the market each day with a sense of confidence or a sense of uncertainty?
- Do you typically feel calm and confident or anxious and panicky when trading?
- Do you view the market as a field of opportunities or a place where market makers have the edge? If you truly believe that the market is out to get you, it will be hard for you to make money. The truth of the matter is that the market is NOT out to get you. But you are what you think; if you truly believe you can't make money trading the markets, you're probably right. So, be positive and try never to think negatively.

Section 3: Questions About Your Time Commitment

This section will help determine what time frame you will be using in your trading. In turn, this will help dictate what type of trader you become (i.e., scalper, day trader, swing trader, short-, intermediate- or long-term trader).

- How much time each day, week or month do you want to put into trading?
- Are you able to put as much time into trading as you would like, or is your work schedule combined with your family life making it impossible to devote as much time as you would like?
- Do you work full-time? If you do, then you obviously can't be a scalper or day trader. A swing to short-term trading would be your best bet here. Don't squeeze day trading into time before work; your family will get upset with you and you will most likely feel pressure to perform. Part-time work is okay if you would like to trade half day; retirees and the semiretired can make one to two trades a day. The fewer the trades a day, the better. Then go do something fun!
- Are you retired, looking to spend two to four hours a day on your trading? If this is the case, you could blend day trading with swing trading.

Section 4: Questions About Your Energy Level

Your energy level doesn't necessarily play a huge role in your overall trading success, but I do think it would be wise to try to match your trading style with your energy level.

For example, many scalpers and day traders tend to have a higher energy level. Swing traders tend to be more even-keeled and are definitely right between higher energy and lower energy. Most people who think of themselves as position traders are those who simply do not have the option of putting a lot of time or energy into their trading.

I don't have any questions for you here, other than, "Are you a more laid-back person, or are you more ADD or ADHD?" I think you will instantly know the answer to this without having to answer any additional questions to see where you fit. If you do have higher than normal energy and it tends to be driven by pressure to perform, that can definitely become a trap and hurt you as a trader. So, really think about this section further and see where you fit in.

Section 5: Questions About Your Capital Commitment

This section will mostly be centered on questions relating to whether you're trading with so-called scared money or risk capital and the amount of money (capital) you're actually using to trade. Money is always emotional, especially when it's tied to your trading, so you need to understand this fully. Let me give you a few questions that you can think about so you can see how this fits into your overall trading plan.

- Will you be trading with scared money—money that's important for paying bills and surviving from day to day? If so, chances are you'll be overly focused on your outcome rather than on your trading-skill development.

- Will you be trading with risk capital? If so, chances are you'll do better than if you're trading with scared money. If you assume you'll lose it all and think of that as a form of tuition, there is no doubt your results will be better.
- Do you feel the urgent need to make trades, whether or not the environment is hospitable? If you do, it's usually because you *have* to make money.
- Do you fail to place a protective stop because you don't want to take an actual loss?
- Do you typically feel stressed when you trade? This could be because it's a money issue, and you need to make money.
- Do you think most of your stress is self-induced? Just remember to set attainable goals and have realistic steps to reach those goals.
- Are you looking consistently to compound your accounts (i.e., IRAs, discretionary)?
- Do you set realistic and achievable trading goals?
- When the market closes each day, do you feel happy or exhausted? Remember always to set reasonable goals; less is more.

Section 6: Questions About Your Wants, Needs and Desires

This section deals with what you ultimately want to get out of your trading or investing. It's really as simple as that.

What you need to do is simply write out exactly what wants, needs and desires you would like to achieve or fulfill through your trading. Let me give you a few questions to help prompt your thinking.

- Are you interested in:
  - Growing your capital base by 20 percent annually? What about 30, 40 or 50+ percent?
  - Conservatively growing your IRA, SEP IRA, 401(k) or any other retirement accounts?
  - Trading for weekly and monthly income to support your lifestyle?
  - Aggressively producing income at a rate of 3.5+ percent a month, which comes to 51+ percent a year?
  - Earning extra money each month to help put your kids through college?
  - Earning extra discretionary income for the family?
  - Making money through your trading for charitable purposes?

After reading through these questions, you've probably gained a better sense of the real, quantifiable goals and desires you have for your trading. Now, what you need to do is write down what you're looking to achieve from your own personal trading—it's really as simple as that. Use the goal-setting guidelines from Chapter 2 to get started.

Going through these **YOU** questions not only helps you determine your **strengths and weaknesses** but it also gives you direction in many different areas on what type of trader you are most suited to become. Take everything you learned in this section and create your own personal objective or STATEMENT by summarizing what you discovered about yourself.

Once again, there are no right or wrong answers here; this was meant to help you think through **critical questions that only YOU can answer about yourself** to help point you in the right direction. This is where many traders go wrong; they simply don't go through these types of exercises, which leads them down the wrong path in their trading. You are now one step ahead of most other traders, so CONGRATULATIONS!

I think this quote by Michael Martin from the book *The Inner Voice of Trading* sums this up beautifully:

> *"Only when you can merge your emotions with your trading rules and combine the trading results with your feelings will you have developed your 'inner voice,' the only 'person' you can count on consistently. You then will have aligned your emotional system with your trading methodology."*

--From *The Inner Voice of Trading* by Michael Martin

TODD MITCHELL

A Final Note from Todd

You did it! You've taken a great first step by not only getting this book but also by reading through its entirety. Great job! Now you know more about trading the markets than 90 percent of the general public does.

You are now well on your way to a brighter future and possibly a new career, if you so choose. If you take the knowledge that you gained from this book and combine it with continued market trading education, the sky is the limit for you and your family. As you learned earlier, you don't need to have an in or a middleman in order to trade profitably, and you certainly don't have to be an expert economist or a financial wizard. You, yourself, with the proper education and training, can trade like the professionals on Wall Street. All it takes is persistence, discipline, hard work, practice, the right mentor and the proper mental attitude.

Let me reiterate, there are many advantages to trading.

- You can work from home.
- You are your own boss.
- You get to choose your trading hours, i.e., what time of day and for how long.
- There are low startup costs.
- You don't need any permits or licenses.
- There's no inventory, no overhead and no employees.

Everything I've provided in this book was shared out of my desire to get you to the next level of trading education. I know firsthand how exciting it is to learn something valuable that you can put to work so you can take charge of your finances and your life. I understand there's an endless amount of information out there on this subject and I encourage you to take it one step at a time. I hope that you make the next move toward realizing your dreams by continuing your trading education.

You have the power to make your dreams come true! Now it's up to you to determine what happens next. I hope to have the opportunity to work with you further in helping you reach your trading goals.

Yours in trading success,

Todd Mitchell

Todd Mitchell

Trading Concepts, Inc.

"One way to keep your momentum going is to constantly seek greater goals."
--Unknown

About Trading Concepts

Since 1994, Trading Concepts has provided investment education and personal mentoring, market analysis, online trading tools and portfolio management techniques to tens of thousands of people from all over the world. Every day, our proven, high-reward trading strategies help traders successfully navigate the markets and chart paths to financial security. At Trading Concepts, we not only stand behind our pledge to provide the highest-quality investment education and trading resources possible, we guarantee it.

Trading Concepts provides practical, step-by-step, easy-to-apply, high-profit, low-risk and low-stress trading plans. The trading strategies found in all of our trading programs are based on proven trading techniques perfected by Todd Mitchell.

Avoiding overly technical or theoretical and complicated material, Trading Concepts presents a practical, balanced approach to trading profitably in today's markets. Since our inception in 1994, we have enriched the lives of an ever-expanding number of students worldwide.

Testimonials

Since 1994, I've had more than 25,000 people ask me to teach them how to trade more successfully. Here are just a handful of students who have taken the time to write to me about their experiences. I have decided to include these here to show you that you can do it too!

***

I wanted to say thank you again for sharing and teaching your methods. Since I have met you, I have not only been able to learn a methodology that will work for the rest of my life, but I have been able to meet other traders who share the same passion as I do. Thank you for being so sincere and committed. I'm sure you know, with the quality of your program, and your commitment to customer service after the sale, you could easily sell your program for three to five times what you do and still sleep well at night. However, it is clear you do what you do out of sincerity and not out of greed. That makes doing business with you feel that much better. Have a good day. – **Michael K.**

After much thought and with a lot of family discussion, I have decided to go full-time trading. I want to thank you for showing me the ropes. I've been diligently following your daily charts since last October. I know fully why your system works. Having spent a lot of time studying complex electrical and economic systems, and knowing a bit about statistics and fractals, I can fully endorse your **trading methodology**. This week I was asked if I was interested in returning to a project manager position at the Electric Power Research Institute. I told the director that I had a better goal. Thanks for sharing your insights with me. – **Jerry M.**

Thank you so much. You've played a pivotal role in my current trading success! I'm now trading full-time and meeting my goals consistently. Thank you!! – **Brian V.**

Your personal approach and commitment to ongoing support are what separate you from all the other services that claim to be dedicated to their students' future success. You really do support your students. Thanks again and feel free to pass this opinion on to others who are considering your trading methodologies. – **Gary D.**

Quite informative ... every day I seem to be "reading" market behavior better and better because of what you have taught me. I'm constantly amazed at the possibilities with your methods. If a trader is patient and does his homework, success is really a possibility with the strategies you teach. For those of us with the discipline to really learn, I think your approach makes so much sense and I continue to see it work day after day. – **Jeff T.**

Everything that I have seen so far is excellent! This is what I have been looking years for. Thank you for sharing this with me. – **Peter**

It now has been three full months since I started to learn how to trade using your course. Your home study course offers trading strategies that are consistently profitable. My trading performance has gone from high risk, large drawdowns and large stops to low risk, low drawdowns and small stops. In other words, I'm profitable and my stress level is way down. Whenever I have a question all I do is give you a call and you're there to answer it.

For anyone who is considering day trading the full or mini S&P 500, who like myself was looking for that magic formula, don't waste your time and money. Todd's course will put you on a path to becoming a better trader than you have ever been. The money is there to be made when you decide you want to learn how to trade for yourself.

Todd, your course is everything one needs to know. Everything you said is true. In these past three months I've been applying your methods and strategies every day. I've seen my trading account consistently rise on a weekly and monthly basis. I've made my mistakes but I'm a much better trader than I've ever been. My next step will be to take your one-on-one training. I thank you for your professionalism and for offering me a chance to become a true TRADER. – **Diego L.**

Trading is going well, up 32 points three days this week!!! Thanks again. – **Glen**

I want to take this opportunity to thank you guys for all you have done for me. It's not often you encounter people who have a profound impact on your life. You guys have done that for me. Again, thank you ... – **Mike R.**

I simply cannot praise it enough. I have spent thousands of dollars for other courses presented by esteemed professionals who did not know how to teach and did not know how to put it together. Thanks a million and good trading to you. God bless you, Todd ... You are a Godsend and a savior to all of us struggling traders. Thanks again. – **Brian L.**

Todd; I have traveled literally all over the country, training one-on-one with some of the best traders and coaches out there. I have also worked on the trading floor of the CME to make certain that I knew the market from the "locals" perspective. I have to say that of all the money and time that I've spent learning various trading methods, I can honestly say that the most valuable and effective trading methodology I have learned is from you. I feel that what you have to offer is simply the best trading methodology that I have found to date. It is not only honest and real, but it works extremely well. I also like the fact that you're not trying to sell me software or trying to be my broker like a lot of people try to do. I like that you're teaching a very real and practical trading method to successfully trade the S&P, or any other market that I choose to trade. Once again, thank you for everything that you've been able to do for me. Talk to you soon. – **Vaughan D.**

I am happy to report that my first week of trading was a profitable one! Even though I was only able to trade three days out of the week, I still made about $200.00! For a beginner I cannot complain. I learned a lot about placing orders and gained a better understanding of recognizing the patterns to trade. I have to admit that the "software" program is a tremendous help. Thanks for all your help! – **Leo**

Thanks and I am learning so much more with your course than with any of the others I have purchased before! – **Lisa P.**

I truly hope these success stories have not only inspired you, but have made you believe that you can do it too!

TODD MITCHELL

Glossary of Terms

Ask price: The price at which the market is prepared to sell a specific instrument. See *Offer*.

Average daily volume: Equals volume for a specified time period divided by the number of business days within that same time period.

Bar chart: A graph of prices, volume and/or open interest for a specified time period used by a chartist to forecast market trends. A daily bar chart typically plots each trading session's high, low and closing price.

Bear: One who expects prices to move lower.

Bear market: A market in which prices are declining.

Bid price: The price at which the market is prepared to buy a specific instrument, opposite of the offer.

Bid/ask spread: The difference between the bid and ask (offer) price.

Breakout: The movement of a market's price through an established support or resistance level.

Broker: An individual or firm that charges a fee or commission for executing buy and sell orders placed by another individual or firm; the role of a broker firm when it acts as an agent for a customer and charges the customer a commission for its services. A full-service broker typically offers market information and advice to assist the customer in trading. A discount broker may simply execute orders for customers.

Brokerage fee: A fee charged by a broker for executing a transaction.

Brokerage house: A firm that handles orders to buy or sell a market on behalf of its customers.

Bull: One who expects prices to move higher.

Bull market: A market in which prices are rising.

Cash account: An account used to hold investor's deposited money for trading.

Charting: The use of charts to analyze market behavior and anticipate future price movements. Typically involves plotting such factors as high, low, closing prices, average price movements and volume.

Chartist: A market analyst who uses charts and graphs of past price movements to predict or anticipate future movements. One who engages in technical analysis and/or uses charting techniques.

Clearinghouse: An entity that settles trades made at an exchange, reconciles clearing member firm accounts each day to ensure that gains have been credited and losses have been collected, and adjusts clearing member firm margins for changing market conditions as appropriate. The clearinghouse may be an independent corporation or exchange-owned.

Close, closing price: The period at the end of the trading session. Sometimes used to refer to the closing price. It is the opposite of the open. The price of the final transaction of the day on any major market.

Closed position: A transaction that leaves the trade with a zero-net commitment to the market with regards to a particular instrument.

Commission: The fee charged by a broker to execute trades and maintain records related to these trades.

Commodities Futures Trading Commission (CFTC): The federal regulatory agency established by the CFTC Act of 1974 to administer the Commodities Exchange Act. There are five CFTC commissioners and they are appointed by the president.

Commodity: Any bulk good traded on an exchange or in the cash (spot) market. Can include foods, meats, metals, grains, energies and lumber.

Commodity Trading Advisor (CTA): An individual or organization that makes recommendations and issues reports on commodity futures or options trading for a fee.

Confirmation statement/customer statement: A statement of a customer's account showing positions and entries. The SEC requires that a customer statement be sent to a customer every time a trade is initiated and closed out.

Congestion: A narrow price range (from high to low) in which a market has been trading for an extended period of time. Many technical analysts consider congestion a sign that a market is getting ready for a strong move. This is the same as consolidation and a sideways market.

Contract: One unit of trading in futures. For example, one contract of wheat trades in units of 5,000 bushels.

Contract month: The designated month in which a particular futures contract may be satisfied by making delivery (the contract seller) or taking delivery (the contract buyer). For example, the S&P 500 contract months are March (H), June (M), September (U), and December (Z).

Day order: An order that is canceled if it's not executed on the day the order is placed.

Day trader: A trader who establishes and liquidates positions within one day's trading, ending the day with no open position in the market.

Day trading: Refers to establishing and liquidating the same position or positions within one day's trading, thus ending the day with no open position in the market.

Double "top," "bottom": A chart pattern formation that signals a possible trend reversal.

Dow Jones Industrial Average (DJIA): A widely used market indicator, composed of 30 large, actively traded issues.

Downtrend: A price trend characterized by a series of lower highs and lower lows.

ECN broker: A type of forex brokerage firm that provides its clients direct access to other forex market participants.

Electronic trading: Trading via computer through an automated order entry and matching system.

Exchange: Any organization, association or group which provides or maintains a marketplace where securities, options, futures or commodities can be traded. Exchanges can also be electronic, as well as physical places. For example, the New York Stock Exchange (NYSE) and the Chicago Mercantile Exchange (CME) are both exchanges.

Exchange traded fund (ETF): An ETF is a basket of securities designed to track an index yet trades like a stock.

Federal funds: Member bank deposits at the Federal Reserve; these funds are loaned by member banks to other member banks.

Federal funds rate: The rate of interest charged for the use of federal funds.

Federal Reserve System: A central banking system in the United States created by the Federal Reserve Act in 1913. It's designed to assist the nation in attaining its economic and financial goals. The structure of the Federal Reserve System includes a Board of Governors, the Federal Open Market Committee and 12 Federal Reserve Banks.

Financial instrument: There are two basic types: (1) a debt instrument, which is a loan with an agreement to pay back funds with interest; (2) an equity security, which is a share of ownership or stock in a company. Derivatives of these basic types are also considered financial instruments. See *Instrument.*

Foreign currency: The currency of a country outside the one in which the trader lives. Both futures and option contracts trade the foreign currencies. Examples are the Australian dollar, British pound, Canadian dollar, the Euro, Japanese yen and the Swiss franc.

Forex market: An over-the-counter market where buyers and sellers conduct foreign exchange business by telephone, computer or other means of communication. Also referred to as foreign exchange market.

Fundamental analysis: The study of basic, underlying factors that will likely affect the supply and demand of the financial instruments being traded in the markets. This type of analysis in commodity markets uses crop reports, weather conditions, unemployment statistics and other similar factors in its analysis. In individual stocks, this type of analysis evaluates the intrinsic value of a stock by evaluating the overall economy, industry conditions and the financial condition of a company. Factors such as these are called the *fundamentals.*

Futures: The term used to designate the standardized contracts covering the sale of commodities for future delivery on a commodity exchange.

Futures contract: A standardized, exchange-traded contract to make or to take delivery of a particular type or grade of commodity at an agreed-upon place and point in the future. Futures contracts are transferable between parties. Examples include wheat, unleaded gas, corn, S&P 500, T-bonds, soybeans and so on.

Futures exchange: A centralized facility for the trading of futures contracts.

Futures market: A continuous auction market in which traders buy and sell commodity and futures contracts for delivery at a specified point in the future. Trading is carried on through open outcry and hand signals in a trading pit.

FX: Foreign exchange market (forex).

Gap: A price area at which the market didn't trade from one day to the next.

Going long: The purchase of a financial instrument for investment or speculation.

Going short: The selling of a financial instrument not owned by the seller, for investment or speculation.

Head and shoulders: A sideways price formation at the top or bottom of the market that indicates a major market reversal.

High: The highest price the market traded at the end of the trading session. It is the opposite of the low.

Initial margin: The total amount of margin per contract required by the broker when a trade position is opened. See *Margin*.

Instruments: Products traded on an exchange or in an over-the-counter market, such as stocks, bonds or futures contracts. See *Financial instrument*.

Last price: The closing price of the last-reported trade on any major market.

Leverage: The use of a smaller amount of capital to control a greater amount of assets. For example, the use of a relatively small amount of cash to trade a market with a relatively high notional value.

Limit order: Orders where you specify a certain price to buy or sell the market. A sell limit order is placed above the current market price and is the lowest price the seller is willing to pay. A buy limit order is placed below the current market price and is the highest price a trader is willing to pay. With certain caveats, you are guaranteed a fill if the market trades through the price you give your broker. If the market merely touches your price, you are NOT guaranteed a fill using this type of order.

Liquid: A characteristic of a financial market with enough units outstanding to allow large transactions without a substantial change in price. Institutional investors are inclined to seek out liquid investments so that their trading activity will not influence the market price.

Liquidity: The ease with which a financial instrument can be bought or sold in the marketplace (converted to cash). A large number of buyers and sellers and a high volume of trading activity are important parts of liquidity. Provides a measure of the level of a market's trading activity, or lack thereof.

Long: To own (buy) a financial instrument. Specifically speaking, the trader wants the price of a market to move up in price so they can sell it back to capture the price difference for a profit. A purchase of three S&P 500 futures contracts would be referred to as *going long* three S&Ps. Long is synonymous with *buying, bought* and *bull market.* The opposite of short.

Lot: The term used to describe a designated number of forex contracts, e.g., a five-lot purchase. Also called "cars."

Low: The lowest price the market traded at the end of the trading session. It is the opposite of the high.

Maintenance margin: The amount of money that must be maintained on deposit at all times. If a customer's equity in any trade position drops to or under the level because of adverse price action, the broker must issue a margin call to restore the customer's equity.

Maintenance performance bond: A sum, usually smaller than the initial margin, which must remain on deposit in the customer's account for any position. A drop in funds below this level requires a deposit back to initial margin levels.

Margin: Funds that must be deposited by a customer with his or her broker, by a broker with a clearing member or by a clearing member with the clearinghouse, for the purpose of insuring the broker or clearinghouse against loss on open trade positions.

Margin account: An account used to hold investor's deposited money for trading that also permits the trader to borrow money from the broker in order to make additional transactions.

Margin call: There are two definitions to this term: (1) a request from a brokerage firm to a customer to bring margin deposits up to minimum levels; and (2) a request by the clearinghouse to a clearing member to bring clearing margins back to minimum levels required by the clearinghouse rules.

Mark-to-market: The daily adjustment of accounts and margin requirements to reflect profits and losses. Positions are mark-to-market.

Market maker: An exchange member whose function is to aid in the making of a market by making bids and offers for his or her account in the absence of or in addition to public buy or sell orders.

Market (entry) order: An order to buy or to sell a financial instrument at the market price the instant that the order is received and processed. When you place a market order, you are saying that you will buy or sell the market at whatever the current price is when your order is processed.

Market-if-touched (MIT) order: A conditional order that becomes a market order when the market reaches a specified price. A sell market-if-touched order is placed above the current market price for entering short on a retracement in a downtrend. A buy market-if-touched is placed below the current market price for entering long on a retracement in an uptrend. These types of orders guarantee a fill if the market just touches the specific price you give your broker. You may experience slippage in the amount of the bid/ask spread because the order is executed as a market order once the condition has been met.

Market price: The current price for which a financial instrument is traded on the market.

Momentum: The tendency of a market to continue movement in a single direction.

Moving averages: A type of technical analysis using the averages of closing prices. A moving average is calculated by adding the prices for a predetermined number of periods and then dividing by the same number of periods.

National Futures Association (NFA): A self-regulatory organization of the commodities futures industry to which all futures exchange members, CTAs and CPOs must belong. The NFA is responsible to the Commodities Futures Trading Commission (CFTC).

Offer: An indication by a trader, investor or dealer to sell a financial instrument. This is the same as the ask price, asking price, quotation or quote. Opposite to the bid.

Open order: Any order resident in the order book, such as a day order or a good-till-canceled order.

Open, opening price: The period at the beginning of the trading session. Sometimes used to refer to the opening price. It is the opposite of the close. The price of the first transaction of the day on any major market.

Option: The right to buy or sell a specified amount of a stocks, bonds or futures contracts at a specified price within a specified time. The right, but not the obligation, to buy or sell the underlying instrument at a specified price within a specified time.

Option buyer: One who purchases an option and pays a premium. Also referred to as the option holder.

Option seller: The person who sells an option in return for a premium and is obligated to perform if the holder exercises his right under the option contract. Also referred to as the option writer.

Order: In most cases, a request for the purchase or sale of an instrument (including execution instructions).

Overbought: A term used by technical analysts that a market has gone up too far (bullish market) and is due for some sort of correction back down. This upside price action doesn't usually match with what the fundamentals are saying.

Oversold: A term used by technical analysts that a market has gone down too far (bearish market) and is due for some sort of correction back up. This downside price action doesn't usually match with what the fundamentals are saying.

Pip: This is the smallest unit of price for any foreign currency. Digits added to or subtracted from the fourth decimal place, i.e., 0.0001. Pips are also called points.

Position: An interest in the market, either long or short.

Position size: The amount of shares or contracts of a financial instrument owned (a long position) or owed (a short position) by a trader.

Position trader: A trader who takes a position in the market, either long or short, and holds the position as a means of speculating on long-term price movements.

Price pattern: A term used by technical analysts to describe a repetitive series of price movements on charts. These chart patterns are used in attempt to predict future movements of a market.

Rally: An upward movement of prices following a decline.

Range: A financial instrument's *high price* minus its *low price* for a particular trading period. A range can be for any trading time period (i.e., three-minute, 15-minute, 30-

minute, 60-minute, daily or weekly charts). For example, subtracting the *low of the day* from the *high of the day* will give you the daily range.

Resistance/resistance line: Technical analysts refer to the term resistance to describe the top (highs) of a market's trading range. When markets approach these levels, they will likely react back down off these highs. Resistance becomes support (see *Support*) when penetrated to the upside. A price area where sufficient supply exists such that the price may have trouble rising above that area.

Retracement: A price move in the opposite direction of a recent trend.

Return (on investment): The percentage profit that one makes, or might make, on one's investment.

Round turn: A round turn counts both the buy and the sell of a trade as one event. From the customer's perspective, a round turn represents two filled orders from his or her brokerage firm—one to take a position and one to offset that position (i.e., same customer, different trades).

S&P 500 Index: An index, with dividends reinvested, of 500 issues representative of leading companies in the U.S. large-cap securities market (representative sample of leading companies in leading industries).

Scalper: Traders who buy and sell numerous shares or contracts during a single trading day in the anticipation of profiting from small price movements. Scalpers rarely carry positions from one day to the next. Their numerous buying and selling throughout the trading day contribute greatly to the liquidity of the markets.

SEC: Acronym for the Securities and Exchange Commission. This government agency jointly regulates U.S. security futures markets with the CFTC.

Security: Common or preferred stock; a bond of a corporation, government or quasi-government body.

Settlement price: The official price at the end of a trading session as determined by the exchange. Also referred to as the *daily settlement price*, except on the last day of trading prior to expiration, in which case it is called the *final settlement price*.

Short: This means to sell (go short) a financial instrument. When using this strategy, a trader wants the price of the market to move down so they can buy the shorted security back to capture the price difference for a profit. A sale of three S&P 500 futures contracts would be referred to as "going short three S&Ps." Short is synonymous with *selling, sold* and *bear market*. The opposite of long.

Sideways trend: Seen in a chart when prices tend not to go above or below a certain range of levels (support and resistance).

Single stock futures (SSF): Futures contracts on individual stocks.

Speculation: The buying or selling of a market for the sole purpose of profiting from those trades and not as a means of protecting other positions.

Speculator: A market participant who tries to profit from buying and selling financial instruments by anticipating future price movements. Speculators assume market price risk and add liquidity and capital to the markets.

Spread: During trading, the difference between the best bid and the best offer for a given financial instrument at a given point in time. Referred to as the bid-offer spread or bid-ask spread.

Stock index: An indicator used to measure and report value changes in a selected group of stocks. How a particular stock index tracks the market depends on its composition, the sampling of stocks, the weighting of individual stocks and the method of averaging used to establish an index.

Stock market: A market in which shares of stock are bought and sold.

Stop orders: An order that becomes a market order when trading occurs at or through your specified price. These can be used to establish a new position, limit a loss on an existing position or protect profits in an existing position. The stop order specifies a price at which an order is to be executed. A sell stop is placed below the market and the buy stop is placed above the market. In a long trade, a sell stop is placed below the market to limit any losses. Also, a buy stop can be placed above resistance to initiate a long trade. Conversely, a sell stop can be placed under support to initiate a short trade. Since stop orders become market orders once touched, your fill price may be beyond your stop price, especially in volatile (fast) markets.

Strike price: The price at which the instrument underlying an options contract can be purchased (if a call) or sold (if a put). Also referred to as the *exercise price*.

Support/support line: Technical analysts refer to the term support to describe the bottom (low) of a market's trading range. When markets approach these levels, they will likely bounce up off these lows. Support becomes resistance (see *Resistance*) when penetrated to the downside. A price area where sufficient demand exists such that the price may have trouble falling below that area.

Technical analysis: An approach to analyzing the financial markets that primarily uses charts for all trading decisions. This approach uses price patterns, rates of change, changes in volume, open interest and various other analysis techniques for making trading decisions. Most technical analysts disregard the fundamentals (see *Fundamental analysis*) altogether.

Ticker: Three- or four-letter symbol used to identify securities listed on the securities exchange on which they trade.

Time conditional order: An order to buy or to sell the market with a time limit set by the customer. Time conditions are typically referred to in the trading industry as:

- **Day order:** An order that remains open until filled, until canceled or until the market closes.
- **Good-till-canceled (GTC) order:** An order that remains open until filled or canceled by the customer.

Trader: A market participant who buys and sells instruments on an exchange or over-the-counter market. See *Day trader*, *Position trader*, and *Scalper*.

Transaction: This term is context dependent. From an operational standpoint, it refers to a matched trade, but has other meanings for clearing and systems purposes.

Treasury bond: U.S. government debt security with a coupon and original maturity of more than 10 years. Interest is paid semiannually.

Treasury note: U.S. government debt security with a coupon and original maturity of one to 10 years.

Trend: The general direction of the market.

Underlying/underlying security: The cash instrument on which a futures or options contract is based.

Unit of trading: The minimum quantity or amount allowed when trading. The normal minimum for common stock is one round lot or 100 shares.

Uptick: This is a new price quote at a price higher than the preceding quote.

Uptrend: A price trend characterized by a series of higher highs and higher lows.

U.S. Equities: Equity of companies listed in the United States.

VIX: The CBOE Volatility Index measures implied market volatility over the next 30 days as derived from prices on S&P 500 Index options. Movement of an asset's total return relative to its mean return over time and is seen as an indicator of total risk.

Volatility: The speed with which the price of a financial instrument rises and falls within a given period of time. When ranges (see *Range*) increase in size (from low to high), the volatility is said to have increased. When ranges decrease in size (from high to low), the volatility is said to have decreased.

Volume: The measure of trading activity traded in a given period.

www.ingramcontent.com/pod-product-compliance
Lightning Source LLC
Chambersburg PA
CBHW071156200326
41519CB00018B/5245